Simply Scones

Also by the authors:
Mostly Muffins
Wild About Brownies

Simply Scones

Leslie Weiner and Barbara Albright

Illustrations by Janet Nelson

ST. MARTIN'S PRESS • NEW YORK

SIMPLY SCONES

Text copyright © 1988 by Leslie Weiner and Barbara Albright.
Illustrations copyright © 1988 by Janet Nelson.
All rights reserved.
Printed in the United States of America. No part of this book may be used or
reproduced in any manner whatsoever without written permission except in the
case of brief quotations embodied in critical articles or reviews. For information,
address St. Martin's Press, 175 Fifth Avenue, New York, N.Y. 10010.

Cover photograph by John Paul Endress
Cover prop styling by Sue Reif
Cover china by Wedgwood

Design by Janet Tingey

LIBRARY OF CONGRESS
Library of Congress Cataloging-in-Publication Data

Weiner, Leslie.
    Simply scones / by Leslie Weiner and Barbara Albright.
        p.   cm.
    ISBN 0-312-01511-9 (pbk.) : $4.95
    1. Scones.   I. Albright, Barbara.   II. Title.
TX770.B55W45   1988   87-27328
641.8'15—dc19   CIP

First Edition

10 9

To our editor, Barbara Anderson,
without whom there would be no book.

To Lowell, Ted, and Lynn,
our tolerant guinea pigs with discriminating tastebuds.

Contents

Metric and Imperial Conversions

All of the recipes in *Simply Scones* were tested using U.S. Customary measuring cups and spoons. Following are approximate conversions for weight and metric measurements. Results may vary slightly when using approximate conversions. Ingredients also vary from country to country. However, we wanted to include this list so you'll be able to make scones wherever you may be.

• VOLUME CONVERSIONS •

U.S. Customary	Approximate Metric Conversion (ml)
⅛ teaspoon	0.5 ml
¼ teaspoon	1.0 ml
½ teaspoon	2.5 ml
1 teaspoon	5.0 ml
1 tablespoon (3 teaspoons)	15.0 ml
2 tablespoons	30.0 ml
3 tablespoons	45.0 ml
¼ cup (4 tablespoons)	60.0 ml
⅓ cup (5⅓ tablespoons)	79.0 ml
½ cup (8 tablespoons)	118.0 ml
⅔ cup (10⅔ tablespoons)	158.0 ml
¾ cup (12 tablespoons)	177.0 ml
1 cup	237.0 ml

◆ LENGTH CONVERSIONS ◆

U.S. Inches	Approximate Metric Conversion (cm)
⅜ inch	Scant 1 cm
½ inch	1.0 cm
⅝ inch	1.5 cm
1 inch	2.5 cm
2 inches	5.0 cm
3 inches	7.5 cm
4 inches	10.0 cm
7 inches	18.0 cm
8 inches	20.0 cm
9 inches	23.0 cm
10 inches	25.0 cm
11 inches	28.0 cm

• COMMONLY USED INGREDIENT CONVERSIONS •

ALL-PURPOSE FLOUR, UNSIFTED AND SPOONED INTO THE CUP

Volume	Ounces	Grams
¼ cup	1.1 oz	31 gm
⅓ cup	1.5 oz	42 gm
½ cup	2.2 oz	63 gm
1 cup	4.4 oz	125 gm

GRANULATED SUGAR

Volume	Ounces	Grams
1 teaspoon	.1 oz	4 gm
1 tablespoon	.4 oz	12 gm
¼ cup	1.8 oz	50 gm
⅓ cup	2.4 oz	67 gm
½ cup	3.5 oz	100 gm
1 cup	7.1 oz	200 gm

FIRMLY PACKED BROWN SUGAR

Volume	Ounces	Grams
1 tablespoon	.5 oz	14 gm
¼ cup	1.9 oz	55 gm
⅓ cup	2.6 oz	73 gm
½ cup	3.9 oz	110 gm
1 cup	7.8 oz	220 gm

Unsalted Butter

Volume	Ounces	Grams
1 tablespoon	.5 oz	14 gm
¼ cup	2.0 oz	57 gm
⅓ cup	2.6 oz	76 gm
½ cup	4.0 oz	113 gm
1 cup	8.0 oz	227 gm

Nuts

Volume	Ounces	Grams
¼ cup	1.0 oz	28 gm
⅓ cup	1.3 oz	38 gm
½ cup	2.0 oz	57 gm
1 cup	4.0 oz	113 gm

Conversions are based on *Nutritive Values of American Foods in Common Units, Agriculture Handbook No. 456*. United States Department of Agriculture. Issued November 1975.

◆ OVEN TEMPERATURE CONVERSIONS ◆

Fahrenheit	Approximate Celsius (Centigrade)
300°F.	150°C.
325°F.	160°C.
350°F.	175°C.
375°F.	190°C.
400°F.	200°C.
425°F.	220°C.
450°F.	230°C.

Introduction: Ensconced in Scones

When we delivered our book proposal to St. Martin's Press, along with samples of assorted scones, the receptionist naturally asked us what we had in the bag. "Scones," we replied. As she watched us unpack she said, "Oh! I thought you said stones." (During the months of recipe testing that followed, we've come to think that sometimes scones can also be stones.) When we offered a scone to another employee standing in the reception area, he declined, saying, "I never eat anything healthy." Not to worry, we thought—scones can sometimes be anything but.

This incident brought to mind an old television episode of "Candid Camera" in which people on the street (we believe it was in the Midwest) were asked, "What is a bagel?" (Keep in mind that this was before bagels were readily available nationwide.) The responses were quite humorous and at least one person thought it was a dog.

Since scones may not yet be a household word (although we predict this will soon change), we decided to ask friends and colleagues that all-important question, "What is a scone?" Here are some of the responses:

Leslie's father-in-law, Paul Weiner, agreed with the popular consensus, "Stones, scones, it's all the same." Another person considered them to be "Scottish muffins." Corinne Imboden, a friend from Indianapolis, said, "It's something British—a kind of sweet bread." When asked what a scone is, Dennis Andes replied, "You go into a diner, you order a scone, you pay about a dollar and you get this little bread thing. That's what a scone is." (Dennis, now you can make them at home.)

Many people did know what scones were, but gave us some interesting descriptions. One person described scones as a cross between a cookie or shortbread and a muffin; another said that scones were a cross between a cookie and a biscuit. For transplanted Englishwoman Helen Kaye, scones are "buttery, floury, moist mouthfuls," and she eats them warm with jam. Janet Burian, a friend who recently returned from a vacation in England and Scotland, described scones as "moist, sweet, flavorful buns." Photographer "Buddy" Endress said they're like "Puffy oatmeal cookies." Barbara's friend, Ted Westray, said that "scones are just muffins that don't have their little cups. You just take the dough and throw it down in a blob on the baking sheet." And, according to "Mr. Webster" (*Webster's Ninth New Collegiate Dictionary*, Merriam-Webster Inc., Springfield, MA, 1986), a scone is "a rich quick bread cut into usually triangular shapes and cooked on a griddle or baked on a sheet."

✦ A SCONE BY ANY OTHER NAME ✦

What is the actual derivation of the word "scone"? As with many other words, sources vary considerably. Here are some of the possibilities:

- ✦ From the Dutch, *schoonbrood:* fine, white bread
- ✦ From the Middle Dutch, *schoon:* bright, and *broot:* bread
- ✦ From the Gaelic, *sgonn:* a shapeless mass or large mouthful
- ✦ From the Middle Low German, *schonbrot:* fine bread
- ✦ Or, the word may be based on the Scottish town of Scone.

In the British Isles, there are many regional variations on the scone theme. These breads/cakes have quite interesting names such as Singing Hinnies, Fat Rascals, and Rock Cakes. And each locale, or household, often has its own specialty.

In Salt Lake City, Utah, the things they call scones are most "unsconelike." They are a fried, puffy yeast dough. These "scones" are often served with honey and butter, and occasionally served as the buns for Sloppy Joes.

• THE TECHNIQUE: HOW TO MAKE PERFECT SCONES •

We find it hard to describe the perfect scone, since they can vary so widely in texture, shape, size, and flavor. Scones should be neither too dry nor too moist. With apologies to the British, we've taken liberties in creating variations on the traditional scones. Our scones vary from cookielike to biscuitlike to cakelike in texture, and from savory to sweet in flavor. But as with wine and other foods, it might be said that "the best" are defined as the ones you like to eat. The following are tips on how to create delicious scones.

Be sure to read each recipe before preparing it, and assemble all the ingredients before starting. This simple procedure (which applies to all recipes) will help avoid many mishaps. When measuring ingredients, be sure to use the appropriate measuring cups for dry and liquid ingredients, and use measuring spoons instead of flatware. Level off measuring spoons with the flat edge of a spatula and read liquid ingredients at eye level.

Making scones is similar to making biscuits—they can be rolled, shaped, or dropped—and the method is about the same. Dry ingredients are mixed together. The chilled butter is cut into the dry ingredients with a pastry blender, or with two knives used scissors fashion, or with fingertips, until the mixture resembles a coarse meal. This helps produce a flaky texture. The liquid ingredients are mixed together and added all at once to the dry ingredients, and then stirred until combined. Some recipes call for kneading the dough several times to develop the "gluten"; however, overkneading the dough will produce a tough scone. A high butter or sugar content in the dough will help inhibit the formation of gluten and produce a more tender product. Depending upon the amount of liquid in the recipe, the consistency of the dough will vary. Some doughs are stiff and can be handled, rolled, and shaped easily; other doughs are wet and sticky, and may need to be dropped, or patted with lightly floured hands.

Use fresh, double-acting baking powder in these recipes. Baking powder can lose its potency if it is stored past its expiration date or if moisture gets into the container. Double-acting baking powder is the most common leavening agent and allows leavening to occur at room temperature and during baking. It contains two acid components, calcium acid phosphate and sodium aluminum sulfate; along with an alkali component, sodium bicarbonate (baking soda); and cornstarch. Adding the liquid to the baking powder starts the chemical reaction between the acid and alkali, forming carbon dioxide and water. Leavening occurs when heat causes the carbon dioxide gas to be released into the batter. In simplified terms, one acid component, calcium acid phosphate, reacts at room temperature, while the other acid component, sodium aluminum sulfate, reacts at oven temperatures. The cornstarch is added to the baking powder to help stabilize the mixture by keeping acid and alkali from reacting during storage.

Baking soda (sodium bicarbonate) is used as the leavening agent to balance the acid-alkali ratio when acid ingredients (such as buttermilk, yogurt, sour cream, citrus juices, and molasses) are included in sufficient amounts in a particular recipe. The acid content of these ingredients can vary, however, and so cream of tartar (an acid salt of tartaric acid) is sometimes added to help ensure sufficient acidity to react with the baking soda. Baking soda and cream of tartar can also be used alone as a substitute for baking powder.

Scones should be baked in a fully preheated oven for the specified length of time or until a cake tester or toothpick inserted into the center of a scone comes out clean. As oven temperatures vary in accuracy, it's best to check the temperature with an oven thermometer.

Cool the scones as directed. For wedge-shaped scones, it's best not to separate the wedges until ready to serve. Cut surfaces tend to dry out quickly and become hard and stale. Scones are best eaten soon after they are baked; however, some cooled scones can be successfully stored in an airtight container at room temperature. Many of the scones also freeze well. Always refrigerate or freeze scones containing meat or cheese, and refrigerate or freeze all scones during the hot summer months.

To reheat scones, wrap them loosely in aluminum foil. Heat room-temperature scones and refrigerated scones at 250°F. for 5 to 10 minutes. Heat frozen scones at 350°F. for 15 to 20 minutes, depending on the size and thickness.

You can create your own scone variations by substituting one type of dried fruit or nut for another. Additions of small amounts of spices such as ground cinnamon, or small amounts of grated orange or lemon peel also work well. Scones with stiff doughs can be shaped into rounds or rolled out and cut into triangles, squares, circles, hearts, diamonds, or other shapes. Stickier doughs are best dropped into mounds on the baking sheet or patted with floured hands into 8- or 9-inch-diameter circles and cut into wedges. For shiny-topped scones, brush the dough with a mixture of an egg yolk, or egg white, or whole egg mixed with ½ to 1 teaspoon of water. (This should be enough egg glaze for two recipes.) For nut-topped scones, brush the dough with the egg glaze, then top with chopped nuts pressed lightly into the dough before baking. (The egg glazes in our recipes are usually optional.) For a cinnamon-sugar topping, brush the dough with ½ to 1 teaspoon of milk, and sprinkle with 1 to 2 teaspoons of granulated sugar mixed with a generous dash of ground cinnamon.

Have fun using our recipes, and creating your own, but beware. According to

English cooking authority Elizabeth David (in *English Bread and Yeast Cookery*, The Viking Press, NY, 1977, p. 529), ". . . once you start on scones where do you stop?"

After testing the recipes for our other two books, *Mostly Muffins* (St. Martin's) and *Wild About Brownies* (Barron's), both of us agree, "Scones are definitely easier and faster to make than either muffins or brownies . . . but they're just as delicious."

Whether you pronounce the word "scone" as 'skōn or 'skän, or even 'stōn, we hope you enjoy scones often.

Sweet Scones

• APPLE OATMEAL SCONES •

Oats, apples, and dates make these hearty scones just right to start the day.

1½ cups all-purpose flour	*1 large egg*
1 cup uncooked old-fashioned rolled oats	*¼ cup milk*
⅓ cup firmly packed dark brown sugar	*2 tablespoons molasses*
2½ teaspoons baking powder	*1 teaspoon vanilla extract*
½ teaspoon salt	*¾ cup diced unpeeled apple*
½ cup unsalted butter, chilled	*⅔ cup chopped pitted dates*

Preheat oven to 375°F. Lightly butter a 10-inch-diameter circle in the center of a baking sheet.

In a large bowl, stir together the flour, oats, brown sugar, baking powder, and salt. Cut the butter into ½-inch cubes and distribute them over the flour mixture. With a pastry blender or two knives used scissors fashion, cut in the butter until the mixture resembles coarse crumbs. In a small bowl, stir together the egg, milk, molasses, and vanilla. Add the milk mixture to the flour mixture and stir to combine. The dough will be sticky.

Stir in the apple and dates until evenly distributed. Spread the dough into an 8-inch-diameter circle in the center of the prepared baking sheet. With a serrated knife, cut into 8 wedges. Bake 22 to 27 minutes, or until a cake tester or toothpick inserted into the center comes out clean. Remove the baking sheet to a wire rack and cool for 10 minutes. Using a spatula, transfer the scones to the wire rack to cool. Recut into wedges, if necessary. Serve warm, or cool completely and store in an airtight container.

Makes 8 scones

• APPLE AND SPICE SCONES •

Delicious served warm with Apple Butter Spread (page 105) and a cup of tea.

1⅔ cups all-purpose flour
½ cup firmly packed dark brown sugar
⅓ cup whole-wheat flour
¾ teaspoon cream of tartar
½ teaspoon baking soda
½ teaspoon salt
½ teaspoon ground cinnamon
⅛ teaspoon ground ginger
Generous dash ground nutmeg

Generous dash ground mace
½ cup unsalted butter, chilled
⅓ cup buttermilk
1 large egg
1 teaspoon vanilla extract
¾ cup chopped dried apples
⅓ cup chopped pecans or walnuts
⅓ cup currants or raisins

Preheat oven to 375°F. Lightly butter a baking sheet.

In a large bowl, stir together the flour, brown sugar, whole-wheat flour, cream of tartar, baking soda, salt, cinnamon, ginger, nutmeg, and mace. Cut the butter into ½-inch cubes and distribute them over the flour mixture. With a pastry blender or two knives used scissors fashion, cut in the butter until the mixture resembles coarse crumbs. In a small bowl, stir together the buttermilk, egg, and vanilla. Add the milk mixture to the flour mixture and stir to combine. The dough will be sticky. Stir in the apples, nuts, and currants until evenly distributed.

Using a ⅓-cup measuring cup, drop the dough onto the prepared baking sheet, leaving about 3 inches between scones. Bake for 20 to 25 minutes, or until a cake tester or toothpick inserted into the center of a scone comes out clean.

Remove the baking sheet to a wire rack and cool for 5 minutes. Using a spatula, transfer the scones to the wire rack to cool. Serve warm, or cool completely and store in an airtight container.

Makes approximately 10 scones

• APRICOT, WHITE CHOCOLATE, AND WALNUT SCONES •

Apricots, white chocolate, and toasted walnuts make a wonderful flavor combination. The heart-shaped variation is perfect for a romantic addition to breakfast in bed. You can shape the scones into heart shapes ahead of time. Wrap the unbaked scones tightly in plastic wrap and aluminum foil and freeze. Bake the still-frozen scone hearts about 20 to 25 minutes.

2 cups all-purpose flour
1/3 cup granulated sugar
2 teaspoons baking powder
1/2 teaspoon salt
1/4 cup unsalted butter, chilled
1/2 cup heavy (whipping) cream
1 large egg

1 1/2 teaspoons vanilla extract
6 ounces white chocolate, cut into 1/2-inch chunks
1 cup toasted coarsely broken walnuts (see Note)
1 cup finely chopped dried apricots

Preheat oven to 375°F.

In a large bowl, stir together the flour, sugar, baking powder, and salt. Cut the butter into 1/2-inch cubes and distribute them over the flour mixture. With a pastry blender or two knives used scissors fashion, cut in the butter until the mixture resembles coarse crumbs. In a small bowl, stir together the cream, egg, and vanilla. Add the cream mixture to the flour mixture and knead until combined. Knead in the white chocolate, walnuts, and apricots.

With lightly floured hands, pat the dough out into a 9-inch-diameter circle in the center of an ungreased baking sheet. With a serrated knife, cut circle into 8 wedges. Bake for 15 to 20 minutes, or until the top is lightly browned.

Remove the baking sheet to a wire rack and cool for 5 minutes. Using a spatula, transfer the scones to the wire rack to cool. Recut into wedges, if necessary. Serve warm, or cool completely and store in an airtight container.

Makes 8 scones

Note: To toast walnuts, place the walnuts in a single layer on a baking sheet and bake at 375°F. for 5 to 7 minutes, shaking the sheet a couple times, until the nuts are fragrant.

Variation: To make scone hearts, on a lightly floured work surface pat out the dough to a thickness of about ⅝ inch. Using a 3¼-inch heart-shaped cookie cutter, cut the dough into hearts. Gather the scraps of dough together and repeat until all the dough has been used to make the hearts. Transfer the hearts to a baking sheet and bake as above. Makes about 9 hearts.

• BANANA CHIP SCONES •

Chip, chip hooray! Three favorites—banana, peanut butter, and chocolate—combine for a heavenly treat.

2 cups all-purpose flour
1/2 cup firmly packed dark brown sugar
2 teaspoons baking powder
1/2 teaspoon baking soda
1/4 teaspoon salt
1/4 cup unsalted butter, chilled

3/4 cup mashed ripe banana
1 large egg
2 tablespoons buttermilk
1 teaspoon vanilla extract
3/4 cup peanut butter chips
3/4 cup semisweet chocolate chips

Preheat oven to 400°F. Lightly grease a 10-inch-diameter circle in the center of a baking sheet.

In a large bowl, stir together the flour, brown sugar, baking powder, baking soda, and salt. Cut the butter into 1/2-inch cubes and distribute them over the flour mixture. With a pastry blender or two knives used scissors fashion, cut in the butter until the mixture resembles coarse crumbs. In a small bowl, stir together the banana, egg, buttermilk, and vanilla. Add the banana mixture to the flour mixture and stir to combine. Stir in the chips. The dough will be sticky.

Spread the dough into an 8½-inch-diameter circle in the center of the prepared baking sheet. With a serrated knife, cut into 8 wedges. Bake for 19 to 21 minutes, or until lightly browned and a cake tester or toothpick inserted into the center of a scone comes out clean.

Remove the baking sheet to a wire rack and cool for 5 minutes. Using a spatula, transfer the scones to the wire rack to cool. Recut into wedges, if necessary. Serve warm, or cool completely and store in an airtight container.

Makes 8 scones

• BANANA MACADAMIA PRALINE SCONES •

Get a taste of the tropics with these jumbo-sized scones. For variety, make the praline with other types of nuts.

¼ cup granulated sugar
2 tablespoons brandy or water
¾ cup lightly salted macadamia nuts or
  walnuts
2½ cups all-purpose flour
⅓ cup firmly packed light brown sugar
2½ teaspoons baking powder
¼ teaspoon salt

⅓ cup unsalted butter, chilled
1 cup mashed ripe banana
2 large eggs
1 teaspoon vanilla extract
2 teaspoons granulated sugar for glaze
  (optional)
Generous dash ground cinnamon for glaze
  (optional)

Lightly oil a 10-inch-diameter circle on a baking sheet. In a small heavy saucepan, stir together the granulated sugar and brandy. Cook over medium heat, stirring constantly, until the sugar dissolves. Increase the heat to high and bring the mixture to a boil. Cook without stirring for 4 minutes, or until the mixture turns amber and caramelizes. Immediately stir in the macadamia nuts and stir to coat the nuts with the syrup. Immediately scrape the mixture onto the prepared baking sheet. Cool for 20 minutes or until hardened. Transfer the mixture to a cutting board and chop the praline.

Preheat oven to 375°F. Lightly butter an 11-inch-diameter circle in the center of a baking sheet.

In a large bowl, stir together the flour, brown sugar, baking powder, and salt. Cut the butter into ½-inch cubes and distribute them over the flour mixture. With a pastry blender or two knives used scissors fashion, cut in the butter until the mixture resembles coarse crumbs. In a small bowl, stir together the bananas, eggs, and vanilla. Add the banana mixture to the flour mixture and stir to combine. The dough will be sticky. Stir in the praline.

Spread the dough into a 9-inch-diameter circle in the center of the prepared baking sheet. Combine the sugar and cinnamon and sprinkle the mixture over the tops of the scones, if desired. With a serrated knife, cut into 8 wedges. Bake for 30 to 35 minutes, or until lightly browned and a cake tester or toothpick inserted into the center of a scone comes out clean.

Remove the baking sheet to a wire rack and cool for 5 minutes. Using a spatula, transfer the scones to the wire rack to cool. Recut into wedges, if necessary. Serve warm, or cool completely and store in an airtight container.

Makes 8 scones

• BLUEBERRY COFFEECAKE SCONES •

These cakelike scones are chock-full of blueberries and covered with a delicious crumb topping. They're great at breakfast and brunch, as well as dessert.

SCONES
2¼ cups all-purpose flour
½ cup granulated sugar
2 teaspoons baking powder
½ teaspoon salt
½ cup unsalted butter, chilled
2 large eggs

¼ cup milk
1 teaspoon vanilla extract
¼ teaspoon grated lemon peel
1½ cups fresh or thawed, drained frozen
   blueberries

CRUMB TOPPING
¾ cup all-purpose flour
¼ cup firmly packed light brown sugar

⅛ teaspoon ground cinnamon
¼ cup unsalted butter, chilled

Preheat oven to 375°F. Lightly butter an 11-inch-diameter circle in the center of a baking sheet.

In a large bowl, stir together the flour, sugar, baking powder, and salt. Cut the butter into ½-inch cubes and distribute them over the flour mixture. With a pastry blender or two knives used scissors fashion, cut in the butter until the mixture resembles coarse crumbs. In a small bowl, stir together the eggs, milk, vanilla, and lemon peel. Add the egg mixture to the flour mixture and stir to combine. The dough will be sticky. With lightly floured hands, gently knead in the blueberries until evenly distributed.

With lightly floured hands, pat the dough into a 9-inch-diameter circle in the center of the prepared baking sheet.

To prepare the topping, in a small bowl stir together the flour, brown sugar, and cinnamon. Cut the butter into ½-inch cubes and distribute them over the flour mixture. With a pastry blender or two knives used scissors fashion, cut in the butter until the mixture resembles coarse crumbs. Sprinkle the topping mixture evenly over the dough to cover. Press crumb topping lightly into the dough. With a serrated knife, cut circle into 8 wedges. Bake for 30 to 35 minutes, until the top is lightly browned and a cake tester or toothpick inserted into the center of a scone comes out clean.

Remove the baking sheet to a wire rack and cool for 15 minutes. Using a spatula, transfer the scones to the wire rack to cool. Recut into wedges, if necessary. Serve warm, or cool completely and store in an airtight container.

Makes 8 scones

• BRAN SCONES •

Great for breakfast! These scones are a nice change from bran muffins and are a good source of fiber.

¼ cup buttermilk
1 large egg
2 tablespoons molasses
1½ teaspoons vanilla extract
¾ cup shredded bran cereal (such as All-Bran)
¼ cup unprocessed bran

1⅓ cups all-purpose flour
¼ cup firmly packed light brown sugar
2 teaspoons baking powder
½ teaspoon baking soda
¼ teaspoon salt
5 tablespoons unsalted butter, chilled

Preheat oven to 375°F. Lightly butter a 9-inch-diameter circle in the center of a baking sheet.

In a medium bowl, stir together the buttermilk, egg, molasses, and vanilla. Stir in the two bran cereals and let stand for at least 2 minutes, or until the cereal is softened. In a large bowl, stir together flour, brown sugar, baking powder, baking soda, and salt. Cut the butter into ½-inch cubes and distribute them over the flour mixture. With a pastry blender or two knives used scissors fashion, cut in the butter until the mixture resembles coarse crumbs. Add the bran mixture to the flour mixture and stir to combine.

With lightly floured hands, pat the dough into an 8-inch diameter circle in the center of the prepared baking sheet. With a serrated knife, cut into 8 wedges. Bake for

17 to 19 minutes, or until the top is lightly browned and a cake tester or toothpick inserted into the center of a scone comes out clean.

Remove the baking sheet to a wire rack and cool for 5 minutes. Using a spatula, transfer the scones to the wire rack to cool. Recut into wedges, if necessary. Serve warm, or cool completely and store in an airtight container.

Makes 8 scones

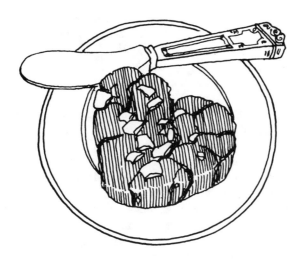

• BROWNIE SCONES •

Chocolaty and nutty scones that are great with a glass of milk.

2 cups all-purpose flour
1/2 cup granulated sugar
1/4 cup firmly packed dark brown sugar
2 1/4 teaspoons baking powder
1/4 teaspoon salt
1/3 cup unsalted butter, chilled
1/3 cup milk

3 ounces unsweetened chocolate, melted
    and cooled to room temperature
1 large egg
1 1/2 teaspoons vanilla extract
1/2 cup coarsely broken walnuts
Additional walnut halves, for garnish
    (optional)

Preheat oven to 350°F. Lightly butter an 8-inch-diameter circle in the center of a baking sheet.

In a large bowl, stir together the flour, sugar, brown sugar, baking powder, and salt. Cut the butter into 1/2-inch cubes and distribute them over the flour mixture. With a pastry blender or two knives used scissors fashion, cut in the butter until the mixture resembles coarse crumbs. In a small bowl, stir together the milk, chocolate, egg, and vanilla. Add the milk mixture to the flour mixture and knead together to combine. Knead in the walnut pieces.

With lightly floured hands, pat the dough into a 7-inch-diameter circle in the center of the prepared baking sheet. With a serrated knife, cut into 8 wedges. Decorate the edge with the walnut halves, if desired. Bake for 17 to 20 minutes, or until a cake tester or toothpick inserted into the center of a scone comes out with just a few crumbs clinging to it.

Remove the baking sheet to a wire rack and cool for 5 minutes. Using a spatula, transfer the scones to the wire rack to cool. Recut into wedges, if necessary. Serve warm, or cool completely and store in airtight container.

Makes 8 scones

• BUTTERMILK SCONES •

Classically delicious. For a new twist, substitute other types of dried fruits for the currants.

2 cups all-purpose flour
⅓ cup granulated sugar
1½ teaspoons baking powder
½ teaspoon baking soda
¼ teaspoon salt

6 tablespoons unsalted butter, chilled
½ cup buttermilk
1 large egg
1½ teaspoons vanilla extract
⅔ cup currants or raisins (optional)

Preheat oven to 400°F.

In a large bowl, stir together the flour, sugar, baking powder, baking soda, and salt. Cut the butter into ½-inch cubes and distribute them over the flour mixture. With a pastry blender or two knives used scissors fashion, cut in the butter until the mixture resembles coarse crumbs. In a small bowl, stir together the buttermilk, egg, and vanilla. Add the buttermilk mixture to the flour mixture and stir to combine. Stir in the currants, if desired.

With lightly floured hands, pat the dough into an 8-inch-diameter circle on an ungreased baking sheet. With a serrated knife, cut into 8 wedges. Bake for 18 to 20 minutes, or until the top is lightly browned and a cake tester or toothpick inserted into the center of a scone comes out clean.

Remove the baking sheet to a wire rack and cool for 5 minutes.

Using a spatula, transfer the scones to the wire rack to cool. Recut into wedges, if necessary. Serve warm, or cool completely and store in an airtight container.

Makes 8 scones

• CARROT NUT SCONES •

While this scone was developed to be nutritious, there is nothing "awfully" healthful tasting about it! Pack one of these scones with a container of yogurt for a lunch that is sure to delight the recipient (and don't forget to pack one for yourself!).

1¾ cups all-purpose flour
¼ cup honey crunch wheat germ
½ cup firmly packed light brown sugar
2 teaspoons baking powder
½ teaspoon baking soda
¼ teaspoon salt
⅛ teaspoon ground cinnamon
Pinch ground mace

¼ cup unsalted butter, chilled
¼ cup plain yogurt
1 large egg
1 teaspoon vanilla extract
1 cup grated carrots
⅔ cup golden raisins
½ cup chopped pecans

Preheat oven to 400°F. Lightly butter a 10-inch-diameter circle in the center of a baking sheet.

In a large bowl, stir together the flour, wheat germ, brown sugar, baking powder, baking soda, salt, cinnamon, and mace. Cut the butter into ½-inch cubes and distribute them over the flour mixture. With a pastry blender or two knives used scissors fashion, cut in the butter until the mixture resembles coarse crumbs. In a small bowl, stir together the yogurt, egg, and vanilla. Add the yogurt mixture to the flour mixture and stir to combine. Stir in the carrots, raisins, and pecans. The dough will be sticky.

Spread the dough into an 8½-inch-diameter circle in the center of the prepared baking sheet. With a serrated knife, cut into 8 wedges. Bake for 19 to 21 minutes, or until the top is lightly browned and a cake tester or toothpick inserted into the center of a scone comes out clean.

Remove the baking sheet to a wire rack and cool for 5 minutes. Using a spatula, transfer the scones to the wire rack to cool. Recut into wedges, if necessary. Serve warm, or cool completely and store in an airtight container in the refrigerator. Let the scones reach room temperature or warm slightly before serving.

These scones freeze well.

Makes 8 scones

• CASHEW SCONES •

Studded with chopped cashews, these scones go well with many of the spreads and butters.

1½ cups all-purpose flour
¼ cup firmly packed dark brown sugar
1½ teaspoons baking powder
¼ teaspoon salt
¼ cup unsalted butter, chilled
1 cup salted, roasted cashews
¼ cup milk
1 large egg

1 teaspoon vanilla extract
3 ounces white chocolate, coarsely chopped
  (optional)
1 egg yolk mixed with ½ teaspoon water
  for glaze
¼ cup whole salted, roasted cashews, for
  garnish (optional)

Preheat oven to 375°F. Lightly butter a baking sheet.

In a large bowl, stir together the flour, brown sugar, baking powder, and salt. Cut the butter into ½-inch cubes and distribute them over the flour mixture. With a pastry blender or two knives used scissors fashion, cut in the butter until the mixture resembles coarse crumbs. Chop the cashews and stir into butter mixture. In a small bowl, stir together the milk, egg, and vanilla. Add the milk mixture to the flour mixture and stir to combine. Stir in white chocolate, if desired. With lightly floured hands, divide the dough into 6 equal-sized pieces (about ⅓ cup each). Shape into balls and press into 3-inch-diameter circles on the prepared baking sheet, leaving about 3 inches between scones. Brush the tops with the egg mixture and top them with the remaining ¼ cup of whole cashews, if desired. Press the nuts lightly into the dough.

Bake for 18 to 23 minutes, or until a cake tester or toothpick inserted into the center of one scone comes out clean.

Remove the baking sheet to a wire rack and cool for 5 minutes. Using a spatula, transfer the scones to the wire rack to cool. Serve warm, or store completely cooled scones in an airtight container.

Makes 6 scones

• CHOCOLATE CHIP ORANGE SCONES •

Chocolate and orange—a classic combination!

2 cups all-purpose flour
1/3 cup granulated sugar
2 teaspoons baking powder
1/2 teaspoon salt
1/2 cup unsalted butter, chilled
2 large eggs

1/4 cup orange juice
1 teaspoon vanilla extract
1/2 teaspoon grated orange peel
3/4 cup miniature semisweet chocolate chips
1 egg white mixed with 1/2 teaspoon water
  for glaze (optional)

Preheat oven to 425°F. Butter a 9-inch-diameter circle in the center of a baking sheet.

In a large bowl, stir together the flour, sugar, baking powder, and salt. Cut the butter into 1/2-inch cubes and distribute them over the flour mixture. With a pastry blender or two knives used scissors fashion, cut in the butter until the mixture resembles coarse crumbs. In a small bowl, stir together the eggs, orange juice, vanilla, and orange peel. Add the egg mixture to the flour mixture and stir to combine. The dough will be sticky. With lightly floured hands, knead in the chocolate chips until they are evenly distributed.

With lightly floured hands, pat the dough into an 8-inch-diameter circle in the center of the prepared baking sheet. If desired, brush the egg mixture over the top and sides of the dough. With a serrated knife, cut into 8 wedges. Bake for 20 to 25 minutes, or until a cake tester or toothpick inserted into the center of a scone comes out clean. Remove the baking sheet to a wire rack and cool for 10 minutes. With a spatula, transfer the scones to the wire rack to cool. Recut into wedges, if necessary. Serve warm, or cool completely and store in an airtight container. These scones freeze well.

Makes 8 scones

• CHOCOLATE-STUFFED PEANUT BUTTER SCONES •

What a fun surprise to find chocolate inside! The combination of chocolate and peanut butter is one of America's favorites. In fact, the three best-selling candy bars all contain peanuts and chocolate in one form or the other. If you're in a hurry, a simpler version of the scone follows.

2 cups all-purpose flour
1/2 cup firmly packed light brown sugar
2 1/2 teaspoons baking powder
1/4 teaspoon salt
1/4 cup unsalted butter, chilled
3/4 cup creamy peanut butter

1/4 cup milk
2 large eggs
2 teaspoons vanilla extract
1/2 cup chopped unsalted peanuts
1 1/2 ounces bittersweet chocolate, broken
   into 8 equal-sized pieces

Preheat oven to 375°F.

In a large bowl, stir together the flour, brown sugar, baking powder, and salt. Cut the butter into 1/2-inch cubes and distribute them over the flour mixture. With a pastry blender or two knives used scissors fashion, cut in the butter until the mixture resembles coarse crumbs. In a small bowl, stir together the peanut butter, milk, eggs, and vanilla. Add the peanut butter mixture to the flour mixture and knead until combined. Knead in the peanuts.

Pat the dough out into a 1/2-inch thickness on a cutting board. Using a floured 2 1/2-to-3-inch-diameter crinkled round biscuit cutter, cut out rounds from the dough. Gather the scraps together and repeat until all the dough is used and there are 16 rounds. Place 8 of the rounds on an ungreased baking sheet. Top each round with a piece of the chocolate and one of the remaining circles of dough. Press the edges gently to seal. Bake for 17 to 19 minutes, or until lightly browned.

Remove the baking sheet to a wire rack and cool for 5 minutes. Using a spatula, transfer the scones to the wire rack to cool. Serve warm or cool completely and store in an airtight container.

Makes 8 scones

Variation: Make the dough as above, omitting bittersweet chocolate, substituting ½ cup unsalted whole peanuts for the chopped peanuts and kneading in ¾ cup of semisweet chocolate chips at the same time. Pat the dough into a 9-inch-diameter circle on a baking sheet. With a serrated knife, cut into 8 wedges. Bake for 20 to 22 minutes, or until a cake tester or toothpick inserted into the center of a scone comes out clean. Cool as above and recut into wedges, if necessary.

• "CLASSIC" CREAM SCONES •

What actually makes a scone "classic" seems to be a matter that calls for clarification. Here is one version that falls into the classification of "classic." These scones are perfect with many of the sweet spreads. Add 1½ teaspoons of grated lemon peel to the dry ingredients as a great way to have lemon with your tea.

2 cups all-purpose flour
¼ cup granulated sugar
2 teaspoons baking powder
⅛ teaspoon salt
⅓ cup unsalted butter, chilled
½ cup heavy (whipping) cream

1 large egg
1½ teaspoons vanilla extract
½ cup currants (optional)
1 egg mixed with 1 teaspoon water for
glaze (optional)

Preheat oven to 425°F. Lightly butter a baking sheet.

In a large bowl, stir together the flour, sugar, baking powder, and salt. Cut the butter into ½-inch cubes and distribute them over the flour mixture. With a pastry blender or two knives used scissors fashion, cut in the butter until the mixture resembles coarse crumbs. In a small bowl, stir together the cream, egg, and vanilla. Add the cream mixture to the flour mixture and stir until combined. Stir in the currants, if desired.

With lightly floured hands, pat the dough into a ½-inch thickness on a lightly floured cutting board. Using a floured 2½-inch-diameter round biscuit cutter or a glass, cut out rounds from the dough and place them on the prepared baking sheet. Gather the scraps together and repeat until all the dough is used. Lightly brush the tops of the scones with the egg mixture, if desired. Bake for 13 to 15 minutes, or until lightly browned.

Remove the baking sheet to a wire rack and cool for 5 minutes. Using a spatula, transfer the scones to the wire rack to cool. Serve warm or cool completely and store in an airtight container.

Makes about 14 scones

• CORN SCONES •

These scones are particularly good when served warm with butter and fruit preserves or honey.

1½ cups all-purpose flour
¾ cup yellow cornmeal
¼ cup firmly packed light brown sugar
2 teaspoons baking powder
¼ teaspoon salt
⅓ cup unsalted butter, chilled

½ cup milk
1 large egg
½ teaspoon vanilla extract
1 egg mixed with 1 teaspoon water for glaze (optional)

Preheat oven to 375°F. Lightly butter a 9-inch-diameter circle in the center of a baking sheet.

In a large bowl, stir together the flour, cornmeal, brown sugar, baking powder, and salt. Cut the butter into ½-inch cubes and distribute them over the flour mixture. With a pastry blender or two knives used scissors fashion, cut in the butter until the mixture resembles coarse crumbs. In a small bowl, stir together the milk, egg, and vanilla. Add the milk mixture to the flour mixture and stir to combine.

With lightly floured hands, pat the dough into an 8-inch-diameter circle in the center of the prepared baking sheet. If desired, brush the egg mixture over the top of the dough. With a serrated knife, cut into 8 wedges. Bake for 15 to 18 minutes, or until the top is lightly browned and a cake tester or toothpick inserted into the center of a scone comes out clean.

Remove the baking sheet to a wire rack and cool for 5 minutes. Using a spatula, transfer the scones to the wire rack to cool. Recut into wedges, if necessary. Serve warm, or cool completely and store in an airtight container.

Makes 8 scones

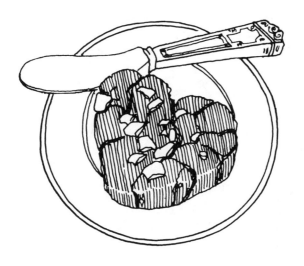

• CRAN-ORANGE SCONES •

So delicious you'll want to keep plenty of frozen cranberries on hand so that you can enjoy these scones year-round.

*½ cup chopped fresh or thawed frozen
   cranberries, drained*
¼ cup plus 2 tablespoons granulated sugar
2 cups all-purpose flour
2 teaspoons baking powder
½ teaspoon salt
½ cup unsalted butter, chilled

2 large eggs
2 tablespoons orange juice
1 teaspoon vanilla extract
½ teaspoon grated orange peel
½ cup chopped pecans
*1 egg white mixed with ½ teaspoon water
   for glaze (optional)*

Preheat oven to 400°F. Lightly butter a 10-inch-diameter circle in the center of a baking sheet.

In a small bowl, stir together the cranberries and 2 tablespoons of the sugar. Let stand about 5 minutes.

Meanwhile, in a large bowl, stir together the flour, remaining ¼ cup sugar, baking powder, and salt. Cut the butter into ½-inch cubes and distribute them over the flour mixture. With a pastry blender or two knives used scissors fashion, cut in the butter until the mixture resembles coarse crumbs. In a small bowl, stir together the eggs, juice, vanilla, and orange peel. Add the egg mixture to the flour mixture and stir to combine. The dough will be sticky. With lightly floured hands, knead in the cranberry mixture and nuts until evenly distributed. With lightly floured hands, pat the dough into a 9-inch-diameter circle in the center of the prepared baking sheet.

Brush the egg white mixture over the top and sides of the dough, if desired. With a serrated knife, cut into 8 wedges. Bake for 20 to 25 minutes, or until a cake tester or toothpick inserted into the center of a scone comes out clean.

Remove the baking sheet to a wire rack and cool for 5 minutes. Using a spatula, transfer the scones to the wire rack to cool. Recut into wedges, if necessary. Serve warm, or cool completely and store in an airtight container.

Makes 8 scones

• DATE-NUT SCONES •

Chock-full of dates and nuts, these scones are yummy topped with Citrus Curd (page 108) or Citrus Butter (page 107).

2¼ cups all-purpose flour
⅓ cup firmly packed dark brown sugar
2¼ teaspoons baking powder
½ teaspoon salt
½ cup unsalted butter, chilled
⅓ cup milk
1 large egg

1 teaspoon vanilla extract
¼ teaspoon grated lemon peel
1 package (8 ounces) chopped pitted dates
½ cup coarsely chopped walnuts
1 egg yolk mixed with ½ teaspoon water
  for glaze (optional)

Preheat oven to 375°F. Lightly butter a 10-inch-diameter circle in the center of a baking sheet.

In a large bowl, stir together the flour, brown sugar, baking powder, and salt. Cut the butter into ½-inch cubes and distribute them over the flour mixture. With a pastry blender or two knives used scissors fashion, cut in the butter until the mixture resembles coarse crumbs. In a small bowl, stir together the milk, egg, vanilla, and lemon peel. Add the milk mixture to the flour mixture and stir to combine. The dough will be sticky. With lightly floured hands, knead in the dates and nuts until evenly distributed.

With lightly floured hands, pat the dough into a 9-inch-diameter circle in the center of the prepared baking sheet. If desired, brush the egg mixture over the top and sides of the dough. With a serrated knife, cut into 8 wedges. Bake for 25 to 30 minutes, or until the top is lightly browned and a cake tester or toothpick inserted into the center of a scone comes out clean.

Remove the baking sheet to a wire rack and cool for 5 minutes. Using a spatula, transfer the scones to the wire rack to cool. Recut into wedges, if necessary. Serve warm, or cool completely and store in an airtight container.

Makes 8 scones

• GINGERBREAD SCONES •

Serve these spicy scones with Maple Butter (page 111) at breakfast or tea.

2 cups all-purpose flour
1/3 cup firmly packed dark brown sugar
2 teaspoons baking powder
1/8 teaspoon baking soda
1/2 teaspoon ground ginger
1/2 teaspoon ground cinnamon
1/8 teaspoon ground cloves
1/8 teaspoon ground nutmeg

1/2 teaspoon salt
1/3 cup unsalted butter, chilled
1 large egg
3 tablespoons molasses
3 tablespoons milk
1 teaspoon vanilla extract
1/2 cup golden raisins (optional)

Preheat oven to 375°F. Lightly butter a 10-inch-diameter circle in the center of a baking sheet.

In a large bowl, stir together the flour, brown sugar, baking powder, baking soda, ginger, cinnamon, cloves, nutmeg, and salt. Cut the butter into 1/2-inch cubes and distribute them over the flour mixture. With a pastry blender or two knives used scissors fashion, cut in the butter until the mixture resembles coarse crumbs. In a small bowl, stir together the egg, molasses, milk, and vanilla. Add the egg mixture to the flour mixture and stir to combine. The dough will be sticky. Stir in the raisins, if desired.

With lightly floured hands, pat the dough into an 8-inch-diameter circle in the center of the prepared baking sheet. With a serrated knife, cut into 8 wedges. Bake 20 to 25 minutes or until a cake tester or a toothpick inserted into the center comes out clean. Remove the baking sheet to a wire rack and cool for 5 minutes. Using a spatula, transfer the scones to the wire rack to cool. Recut into wedges, if necessary. Serve warm.

Makes 8 scones

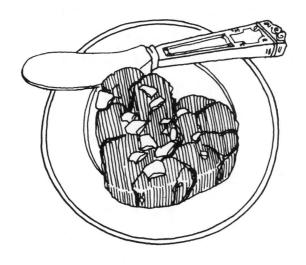

• GRANOLA SCONES •

Made with homemade granola, these scones can make any breakfast special. You'll also have leftover granola to munch on for snacks.

CRUNCHY GRANOLA
1⅓ cups uncooked old-fashioned rolled oats
⅓ cup shredded coconut
¼ cup lightly salted hulled sunflower seeds
¼ cup coarsely chopped walnuts
¼ cup coarsely chopped pecans
¼ cup slivered almonds

¼ cup unsalted butter
¼ cup honey
¼ teaspoon vanilla extract
½ cup raisins
¼ cup chopped pitted dates

SCONES
1⅔ cups all-purpose flour
⅓ cup whole-wheat flour
¼ cup firmly packed dark brown sugar
2¼ teaspoons baking powder
¼ teaspoon salt

⅓ cup unsalted butter, chilled
⅓ cup milk
1 large egg
1 teaspoon vanilla extract
1½ cups Crunchy Granola

To prepare the granola:
Preheat oven to 350°F. Lightly butter a 13-by-10-inch jelly-roll pan.

In a large bowl, combine the oats, coconut, sunflower seeds, and nuts. In a medium saucepan, combine the butter and honey. Cook over medium heat, stirring often, until the butter is melted and the mixture is hot. Remove the pan from the heat and stir in the vanilla. Add the oat mixture to the saucepan and stir to coat. Spread the mixture in an even layer in the prepared pan. Bake for 13 to 18 minutes, or until the mixture is lightly toasted and golden brown. Stir the mixture twice during baking. Remove the baking pan to a wire rack and cool for 5 minutes. Remove the granola to a large bowl and cool for about 30 minutes, or until mixture reaches room temperature, stirring occasionally. When the granola is completely cooled, stir in the dried fruits.

Makes about 4¼ cups

To prepare the scones:
Preheat oven to 375°F. Lightly butter a baking sheet.

In a large bowl, stir together the flours, brown sugar, baking powder, and salt. Cut the butter into ½-inch cubes and distribute them over the flour mixture. With a pastry blender or two knives used scissors fashion, cut in the butter until the mixture resembles coarse crumbs. In a small bowl, stir together the milk, egg, and vanilla. Add the milk mixture to the flour mixture and stir to combine. The dough will be slightly sticky. With lightly floured hands, knead in the granola until evenly distributed.

Using a ⅓-cup measuring cup, drop the dough onto the prepared baking sheet, leaving about 3 inches between scones. Bake for 20 to 25 minutes, until a cake tester or toothpick inserted into the center of a scone comes out clean.

Remove the baking sheet to a wire rack and cool for 5 minutes. Using a spatula, transfer the scones to the wire rack to cool. Serve warm, or cool completely and store in an airtight container.

Makes approximately 8 scones

• HAZELNUT CHOCOLATE CHIP SCONES •

These cakey scones are studded with hazelnuts and chocolate chips. They're great with a mug of steaming hot cocoa.

2 cups all-purpose flour
1/3 cup firmly packed dark brown sugar
1 1/2 teaspoons baking powder
1/2 teaspoon baking soda
1/4 teaspoon salt
6 tablespoons unsalted butter, chilled
1/2 cup buttermilk

1 large egg
1 1/2 teaspoons vanilla extract
1 cup semisweet or milk chocolate chips
1/2 cup toasted hazelnuts (see Note)
Additional toasted hazelnuts for garnish
  (optional)

Preheat oven to 400°F. Lightly butter a 9-inch-diameter circle in the center of the baking sheet.

In a large bowl, stir together the flour, brown sugar, baking powder, baking soda, and salt. Cut the butter into 1/2-inch cubes and distribute them evenly over the flour mixture. With a pastry blender or two knives used scissors fashion, cut in the butter until the mixture resembles coarse crumbs. In a small bowl, stir together the buttermilk, egg, and vanilla. Add the buttermilk mixture to the flour mixture and stir to combine. Stir in the chocolate chips and hazelnuts. The dough will be sticky.

Spread the dough into an 8-inch-diameter circle in the center of the prepared baking sheet. Arrange additional hazelnuts around the edge of the dough for garnish, if desired. With a serrated knife, cut into 8 wedges. Bake for 17 to 19 minutes, or until the top is lightly browned and a cake tester or toothpick inserted into the center of a scone comes out clean.

Remove the baking sheet to a wire rack and cool for 5 minutes. Using a spatula, transfer the scones to the wire rack to cool. Recut into wedges, if necessary. Serve warm, or cool completely and store in an airtight container.

Makes 8 scones

Note: To toast hazelnuts, place the hazelnuts in a single layer on a baking sheet and bake at 350°F. for about 12 minutes, shaking the sheet a couple of times until the nuts are golden beneath the skins. Wrap the nuts in a clean kitchen towel. Cool for 20 minutes and rub off the skins.

· JAM-FILLED WALNUT SCONES ·

Starwberry preserves add color to the centers of these small-sized treats. Try other flavors of preserves with these cookielike scones.

2 cups all-purpose flour
1/2 cup very finely chopped walnuts
1/4 cup granulated sugar
2 teaspoons baking powder
1/2 teaspoon baking soda

1/4 teaspoon salt
6 tablespoons unsalted butter, chilled
2/3 cup buttermilk
1 teaspoon vanilla extract
1/4 cup strawberry preserves

Preheat oven to 400°F. Lightly butter a baking sheet.

In a large bowl, stir together the flour, walnuts, sugar, baking powder, baking soda, and salt. Cut the butter into 1/2-inch cubes and distribute them over the flour mixture. With a pastry blender or two knives used scissors fashion, cut in the butter until the mixture resembles coarse crumbs. In a small bowl, stir together the buttermilk and vanilla. Add the buttermilk mixture to the flour mixture and stir to combine.

With lightly floured hands, divide the dough into two equal-sized pieces and pat each portion into a 5-inch circle on a lightly floured cutting board. Cut each circle into 6 wedges. Transfer the 12 pieces to the prepared baking sheet. Dip the point of a sharp knife in flour and make a slit in the top of each scone, dipping the knife in flour as needed. Carefully spoon 1 teaspoon of strawberry preserves into the slit in the top of each scone. Bake for 17 to 19 minutes, or until the tops are lightly browned.

Remove the baking sheet to a wire rack and cool for 5 minutes. Using a spatula, transfer the scones to the wire rack to cool. Serve warm, or cool completely and store in a single layer in an airtight container.

These scones freeze well.

Makes 12 scones

• MOCHA CHIP COOKIE SCONES •

Somewhere between a giant cookie and a scone, these rich scones flecked with bittersweet chocolate are best served at dessert or snack time. They're especially delicious topped with Chocolate Cream Cheese (page 106) or White Chocolate Cream Cheese (page 113).

1¾ cups all-purpose flour
½ cup granulated sugar
1 tablespoon non-alkalized unsweetened
    cocoa powder
2½ teaspoons instant espresso powder
1 teaspoon cream of tartar
¾ teaspoon baking soda

½ teaspoon salt
⅓ cup unsalted butter, chilled
⅓ cup buttermilk
1 large egg
1½ teaspoons vanilla extract
6 ounces finely chopped bittersweet
    chocolate (see Note)

Preheat oven to 375°F. Lightly butter a baking sheet.

In a large bowl, stir together the flour, sugar, cocoa, espresso powder, cream of tartar, baking soda, and salt.

Cut the butter into ½-inch cubes and distribute them over the flour mixture. With a pastry blender or two knives used scissors fashion, cut in the butter until the mixture resembles coarse crumbs. In a small bowl, stir together the buttermilk, egg, and vanilla. Add the milk mixture to the flour mixture and stir to combine. The dough will be very sticky. Stir in the chocolate until evenly distributed.

Using a ⅓-cup measuring cup, drop the dough onto the prepared baking sheet, leaving about 4 inches between scones. Bake for 25 to 30 minutes, or until a cake tester or toothpick inserted into the center of a scone comes out clean. Remove the baking sheet to a wire rack and cool for 5 minutes. Using a spatula, transfer the scones to the wire rack to cool. Serve warm or cool completely and store in an airtight container.

Makes approximately 8 scones

Note: The chocolate can be chopped by processing in a food processor fitted with a steel blade.

◆ "MUDPIE" SCONES ◆

While these scones are reminiscent in appearance of a favorite childhood creation, one bite lets you know these scones speak *chocolate* loud and clear. Using milk chocolate bars containing fruit and nuts adds flavor complexity with a minimum amount of work. A glass of cold milk is the perfect accompaniment to these rich scones.

2 cups all-purpose flour
½ cup firmly packed light brown sugar
⅓ cup non-alkalized cocoa powder
2 teaspoons baking powder
¼ teaspoon salt
6 tablespoons unsalted butter, chilled
½ cup milk

1 large egg
1 teaspoon vanilla extract
2 bars (5 ounces each) fruit and nut milk
 chocolate, cut into ¼- to ½-inch pieces
Confectioners sugar, for dusting the tops of
 the scones (optional)

Preheat oven to 375°F. Lightly butter a baking sheet.

In a large bowl, stir together the flour, brown sugar, cocoa, baking powder, and salt. Cut the butter into ½-inch cubes and distribute them over the flour mixture. With a pastry blender or two knives used scissors fashion, cut in the butter until the mixture resembles coarse crumbs. In a small bowl, stir together the milk, egg, and vanilla. Add the milk mixture to the flour mixture and stir to combine. Stir in the chocolate chunks.

Using a ⅓-cup measuring cup, drop the dough onto the prepared baking sheet, leaving about 3 inches between scones. Bake for 16 to 18 minutes, or until a cake tester or toothpick inserted into the center of a scone comes out clean.

Remove the baking sheet to a wire rack and cool for 5 minutes. Using a spatula, transfer the scones to the wire rack to cool. Serve warm, or cool completely and store in an airtight container. Dust with confectioners sugar, if desired.

Makes approximately 9 scones

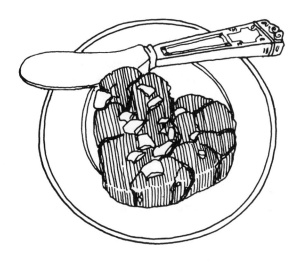

• NUTTY SCONES •

Chock-full of nuts, these crunchy scones are a great addition to any breakfast.

2¼ cups all-purpose flour
½ cup firmly packed dark brown sugar
2 teaspoons baking powder
½ teaspoon salt
½ cup unsalted butter, chilled
2 large eggs
¼ cup milk
1 teaspoon vanilla extract

1½ cups coarsely chopped assorted nuts
such as a combination of cashews,
pecans, Brazil nuts, walnuts, and
toasted almonds (see Note)
½ cup chopped dried apricots or papaya
¼ cup shredded coconut
1 egg white mixed with ½ teaspoon water
for glaze (optional)

Preheat oven to 425°F. Butter a 10-inch-diameter circle in the center of a baking sheet.

In a large bowl, stir together the flour, brown sugar, baking powder, and salt. Cut the butter into ½-inch cubes and distribute them over the flour mixture. With a pastry cutter or two knives used scissors fashion, cut in the butter until the mixture resembles coarse crumbs. In a small bowl, stir together the eggs, milk, and vanilla. Add the egg mixture to the flour mixture and stir to combine. The dough will be sticky. With lightly floured hands, knead in the nuts, apricots, and coconut until they are evenly distributed.

With lightly floured hands, pat the dough into a 9-inch-diameter circle in the center of the prepared baking sheet. If desired, brush the egg mixture over the top and sides of the dough. With a serrated knife, cut into 8 wedges. Bake for 20 to 25 minutes, or until a cake tester or toothpick inserted into the center of a scone comes out clean.

Remove the baking sheet to a wire rack and cool for 10 minutes. With a spatula, transfer the scones to the wire rack to cool. Serve warm, or cool completely and store in an airtight container. Recut into wedges, if necessary.

These scones freeze well.

Makes 8 scones

Note: For best results, use at least 4 types of assorted nuts in the recipe. Some may be lightly salted. To toast almonds, place in a single layer on a baking sheet or jelly-roll pan. Bake at 350°F. for 6 to 7 minutes, stirring once or twice, until lightly browned.

• OAT CURRANT SCONES •

Classic scones that are delicious with fruit jam and stiffly whipped heavy cream.

2 cups all-purpose flour
1 cup uncooked old-fashioned rolled oats
1/4 cup granulated sugar
1 tablespoon baking powder
1/2 teaspoon salt
1/4 teaspoon cream of tartar

1/2 cup unsalted butter, chilled
1/3 cup heavy (whipping) cream
2 large eggs
1 1/2 teaspoons vanilla extract
1/2 cup currants
1/2 cup chopped walnuts

Preheat oven to 425°F.

In a large bowl, stir together the flour, oats, sugar, baking powder, salt, and cream of tartar. Cut the butter into 1/2-inch cubes and distribute them over the flour mixture. With a pastry blender or two knives used scissors fashion, cut in the butter until the mixture resembles coarse crumbs. In a small bowl, stir together the cream, eggs, and vanilla. Add the cream mixture to the flour mixture and stir to combine. Stir in the currants and walnuts.

With lightly floured hands, pat the dough into an 8-inch-diameter circle in the center of an ungreased baking sheet. With a serrated knife, cut into 8 wedges. Bake for 15 to 17 minutes, or until the top is lightly browned and a cake tester or toothpick inserted into the center of a scone comes out clean.

Remove the baking sheet to a wire rack and cool for 5 minutes. Using a spatula, transfer the scones to the wire rack to cool. Recut into wedges, if necessary. Serve warm, or cool completely and store in an airtight container.

Makes 8 scones

• ORANGE DATE STOVE-TOP SCONES •

A great accompaniment for breakfast when served hot from the griddle.

1¾ cups all-purpose flour
½ cup granulated sugar
¾ teaspoon baking powder
½ teaspoon salt
¼ teaspoon baking soda
½ cup unsalted butter, chilled

1 large egg
2 tablespoons milk
¼ teaspoon grated orange peel
¼ teaspoon vanilla extract
⅔ cup chopped pitted dates

In a large bowl, stir together the flour, sugar, baking powder, salt, and baking soda. Cut butter into ½-inch cubes and distribute them over the flour mixture. With a pastry blender or two knives used scissors fashion, cut in the butter until the mixture resembles coarse crumbs. In a small bowl, stir together the egg, milk, orange peel, and vanilla. Add the egg mixture to the flour mixture and stir to combine. With lightly floured hands, knead in the dates.

With a lightly floured rolling pin on a lightly floured surface, roll out the dough to a ⅜-inch thickness. Cut into 2-inch-diameter circles. Reroll the scraps and repeat the procedure with the remaining dough.

Heat a lightly oiled, large skillet over medium heat until drops of water sizzle when dropped onto the skillet. Cook for 5 to 7 minutes on each side, or until lightly browned and a cake tester or toothpick inserted into the center of a scone comes out clean.

Using a spatula, transfer scones to a wire rack to cool. Serve warm, or cool completely and store in an airtight container. These scones are best served warm.

Makes approximately 16 scones

• ORANGE POPPY SEED SCONES •

The perfect accompaniment for luncheon salads.

2¼ cups all-purpose flour
½ cup granulated sugar
¼ cup poppy seeds
1 teaspoon cream of tartar
¾ teaspoon baking soda
½ teaspoon salt

½ cup unsalted butter, chilled
¼ cup orange juice
1 large egg
¼ teaspoon grated orange peel
1 egg white mixed with ½ teaspoon water
   for glaze (optional)

Preheat oven to 375°F. Lightly butter a 10-inch-diameter circle in the center of a baking sheet.

In a large bowl, stir together the flour, sugar, poppy seeds, cream of tartar, baking soda, and salt. Cut the butter into ½-inch cubes and distribute them over the flour mixture. With a pastry blender or two knives used scissors fashion, cut in the butter until the mixture resembles coarse crumbs. In a small bowl, stir together the juice, egg, and orange peel. Add the juice mixture to the flour mixture and stir to combine. The dough will be sticky.

With lightly floured hands, pat the dough into a 9-inch-diameter circle in the center of the prepared baking sheet. If desired, brush the egg mixture over the top of the dough. With a serrated knife, cut into 8 wedges. Bake for 20 to 25 minutes, or until the top is lightly browned and a cake tester or toothpick inserted into the center of a scone comes out clean.

Remove the baking sheet to a wire rack and cool for 5 minutes. Using a spatula, transfer the scones to the wire rack to cool. Recut into wedges, if necessary. Serve warm, or cool completely and store in an airtight container.

Makes 8 scones

• PISTACHIO FIG SCONES •

Pistachio nuts and chopped figs blend to create a sophisticated taste combination. Served with Pistachio Honey Spread (page 111), these scones are sure to create a sensation at your next brunch.

1¼ cups all-purpose flour	1 large egg
3 tablespoons firmly packed light brown sugar	2 tablespoons milk
	½ teaspoon vanilla extract
1¼ teaspoons baking powder	⅓ cup shelled pistachio nuts or slivered almonds
¼ teaspoon salt	
⅓ cup unsalted butter, chilled	⅓ cup chopped trimmed figs

Preheat oven to 375°F. Lightly butter a baking sheet.

In a large bowl, stir together the flour, brown sugar, baking powder, and salt. Cut butter into ½-inch cubes and distribute them over the flour mixture. With a pastry blender or two knives used scissors fashion, cut in the butter until the mixture resembles coarse crumbs. In a small bowl, stir together the egg, milk, and vanilla. Add the egg mixture to the flour mixture and stir to combine. The dough will be sticky. Stir in the nuts and figs until evenly distributed.

Using a ⅓-cup measuring cup, drop the dough onto the prepared baking sheet, leaving about 3 inches between scones. Bake for 20 to 25 minutes, or until a cake tester or toothpick inserted into the center of a scone comes out clean.

Remove the baking sheet to a wire rack and cool for 5 minutes. Using a spatula, transfer the scones to the wire rack to cool. Serve warm, or cool completely and store in an airtight container.

Makes approximately 6 scones

• PLUM ALMOND SCONES •

Pieces of fresh plums add flavor and moisture to these summertime scones.

2 cups all-purpose flour
1/3 cup firmly packed light brown sugar
1 1/2 teaspoons baking powder
1/2 teaspoon baking soda
1/4 teaspoon salt
6 tablespoons unsalted butter, chilled

1/2 cup plain yogurt
1 large egg
1 1/2 teaspoons vanilla extract
2/3 cup chopped plums (2 to 4 firm fresh plums)
1/2 cup slivered blanched almonds, toasted (see Note)

Preheat oven to 400°F. Lightly butter a baking sheet.

In a large bowl, stir together the flour, brown sugar, baking powder, baking soda, and salt. Cut the butter into 1/2-inch cubes and distribute them over the flour mixture. With a pastry blender or two knives used scissors fashion, cut in the butter until the mixture resembles coarse crumbs. In a small bowl, stir together the yogurt, egg, and vanilla. Add the yogurt mixture to the flour mixture and stir to combine. Stir in the chopped plums and almonds until they are evenly distributed.

Using a 1/4-cup measuring cup, drop the dough onto the prepared baking sheet, leaving about 2 inches between scones. Bake for 15 to 17 minutes, or until the tops are lightly browned and a cake tester or toothpick inserted into the center of a scone comes out clean.

Remove the baking sheet to a wire rack and cool for 5 minutes. Using a spatula, transfer the scones to the wire rack to cool. Serve warm, or cool completely and store in an airtight container.

Makes approximately 12 scones

Note: To toast almonds, place the almonds in a single player on a baking sheet and bake at 375°F. for 5 to 7 minutes, shaking the sheet a couple times, until the nuts are lightly browned.

• PRALINE AND CREAM SCONES •

Even great for dessert!

¼ cup granulated sugar
2 tablespoons rum or water
¾ cup pecans
2¼ cups all-purpose flour
⅓ cup firmly packed light brown sugar
2 teaspoons baking powder
½ teaspoon salt

⅓ cup unsalted butter, chilled
2 large eggs
¼ cup heavy (whipping) cream
1 teaspoon vanilla extract
1 egg yolk mixed with ½ teaspoon water
* for glaze*
16 pecan halves for garnish

Lightly oil a 10-inch-diameter circle on a baking sheet. In a small heavy saucepan, stir together the granulated sugar and rum. Cook over medium heat, stirring constantly, until the sugar dissolves. Increase the heat to high and bring the mixture to a boil. Cook without stirring for 4 minutes, or until the mixture turns amber and caramelizes. Immediately stir in the pecans and stir to coat the nuts with the syrup. Immediately scrape the mixture onto the prepared baking sheet. Cool for 20 minutes or until hardened. Transfer the mixture to a cutting board and chop the praline.

Preheat oven to 400°F. Lightly butter a 10-inch-diameter circle in the center of a baking sheet.

In a large bowl, stir together the flour, brown sugar, baking powder, and salt. Cut the butter into ½-inch cubes and distribute them over the flour mixture. With a pastry blender or two knives used scissors fashion, cut in the butter until the mixture resembles coarse crumbs. In a small bowl, stir together the eggs, cream, and vanilla.

Add the egg mixture to the flour mixture and stir to combine. The dough will be sticky. With lightly floured hands, knead in the praline until evenly distributed.

With lightly floured hands, pat the dough into a 9-inch-diameter circle in the center of the prepared baking sheet. Brush the egg mixture over the top and sides of the dough. With a serrated knife, cut into 8 wedges. Press 2 pecan halves onto the end of each wedge. Bake for 20 to 25 minutes, or until a cake tester or toothpick inserted into the center of a scone comes out clean.

Remove the baking sheet to a wire rack and cool for 10 minutes. Using a spatula, transfer the scones to the wire rack to cool. Recut into wedges, if necessary. Serve warm, or cool completely and store in an airtight container.

These scones freeze well.

Makes 8 scones

• PRUNE AND ARMAGNAC SCONES •

We've borrowed the classic French combination of Armagnac and prunes and used it to flavor these Americanized drop scones. For extra richness and flavor complexity, add chopped bittersweet chocolate!

1 cup chopped pitted prunes
⅓ cup Armagnac brandy
2 cups all-purpose flour
⅓ cup firmly packed light brown sugar
2 teaspoons baking powder
¼ teaspoon salt
⅓ cup unsalted butter, chilled

⅓ cup milk
1 large egg
1 teaspoon vanilla extract
¾ cup chopped walnuts
3 ounces finely chopped bittersweet
    chocolate (optional)

In a small saucepan, combine the prunes and Armagnac. Bring the mixture to a boil, stirring occasionally. Remove the pan from the heat and let the mixture stand for 30 minutes.

Preheat oven to 400°F. Lightly butter a baking sheet.

In a large bowl, stir together the flour, brown sugar, baking powder, and salt. Cut the butter into ½-inch cubes and distribute them evenly over the flour mixture. With a pastry blender or two knives used scissors fashion, cut in the butter until the mixture resembles coarse crumbs. In a small bowl, stir together the Armagnac/prune mixture, milk, egg, and vanilla. Add the prune mixture to the flour mixture and stir to combine. Stir in the walnuts and chocolate, if desired.

Using a ⅓-cup measuring cup, drop the dough onto the prepared baking sheet, leaving about 2 inches between scones. Bake for 17 to 20 minutes, or until the tops are lightly browned and a cake tester or toothpick inserted into the center of a scone comes out clean.

Remove the baking sheet to a wire rack and cool for 5 minutes. Using a spatula, transfer the scones to the wire rack to cool. Serve warm, or cool completely and store in an airtight container.

These scones freeze well.

Makes approximately 9 scones

• RAISIN BRAN SCONES •

The mild nutty flavor makes these scones a perfect accompaniment to jams and jellies, as well as many of our spreads and butters.

1½ cups raisin bran cereal
½ cup milk
2 cups all-purpose flour
½ cup firmly packed dark brown sugar
2 teaspoons baking powder
½ teaspoon salt

½ cup unsalted butter, chilled
2 large eggs
1½ teaspoons vanilla extract
⅔ cup coarsely chopped walnuts
1 egg white mixed with ½ teaspoon water
    for glaze (optional)

Preheat oven to 375°F. Butter a 10-inch-diameter circle in the center of a baking sheet.

In a small bowl, stir together the cereal and milk. Let mixture stand for 5 to 10 minutes to soften.

In a large bowl, stir together the flour, brown sugar, baking powder, and salt. Cut the butter into ½-inch cubes and distribute them over the flour mixture. With a pastry blender or two knives used scissors fashion, cut in the butter until the mixture resembles coarse crumbs. Stir the eggs and vanilla into the cereal mixture. Add the cereal mixture to the flour mixture and stir to combine. The dough will be sticky. With lightly floured hands, knead in the nuts until they are evenly distributed.

With lightly floured hands, pat the dough into a 9-inch-diameter circle in the center of the prepared baking sheet. If desired, brush the egg mixture over the top and sides of the dough. With a serrated knife, cut into 8 wedges. Bake for 30 to 35 minutes, or until a cake tester or toothpick inserted in the center of a scone comes out clean.

Remove the baking sheet to a wire rack and cool for 10 minutes. Using a spatula, transfer the scones to the wire rack to cool. Recut into wedges, if necessary. Serve warm, or cool completely and store in an airtight container.

Makes 8 scones

• RASPBERRY-FILLED ALMOND SCONES •

Raspberry preserves sandwiched between layers of almond-coconut scones to create a special treat.

2 cups all-purpose flour
2 tablespoons granulated sugar
2 teaspoons baking powder
½ teaspoon salt
½ cup shredded coconut
⅓ cup almond paste (about 3½ ounces), well chilled
¼ cup unsalted butter, chilled

⅓ cup milk
1 large egg
½ teaspoon vanilla extract
¼ teaspoon almond extract
1½ tablespoons seedless raspberry preserves
1 egg yolk mixed with ½ teaspoon water for glaze
3 tablespoons slivered almonds

Preheat oven to 375°F. Lightly butter a baking sheet.

In a large bowl, stir together the flour, sugar, baking powder, and salt. Place the coconut in the container of a food processor fitted with a steel blade. Process for 30 seconds, or until the coconut is finely chopped. Stir the coconut into the flour mixture. Cut the almond paste and butter into ½-inch pieces and distribute them over the flour mixture. With a pastry blender or two knives used scissors fashion, cut in the almond paste and butter until the mixture resembles coarse crumbs. In a small bowl, stir together the milk, egg, and vanilla and almond extracts. Add the milk mixture to the flour mixture and stir to combine.

Pat the dough out into a ⅜-inch thickness on a lightly floured cutting board. Using a floured 2½-inch-diameter round biscuit cutter, cut out rounds from the dough.

Gather the scraps together and repeat until all the dough is used and there are 18 rounds. Place 9 of the rounds on the prepared baking sheet, leaving about 3 inches between scones. Mound ½ teaspoon of preserves in the center of each round. Top each round with one of the remaining circles of dough. Press the edges together to seal well. Brush the top and sides with the egg mixture and top each with 1 teaspoon of almonds. Press the nuts lightly into the dough. Bake for 17 to 22 minutes, or until the tops are just lightly browned and the bottoms are browned.

Remove the baking sheet to a wire rack and cool for 5 minutes. Using a spatula, transfer the scones to the wire rack to cool. Serve warm, or cool completely and store in an airtight container.

Makes 9 scones

· SCONES A LA FLORENCE ·

Inspired by Pane del Pescatore (bread of the fisherman), a sconelike bread from Il Fornaio, a bakery off the Ponte Vecchio in Florence, Italy, these scones are filled with raisins and topped with pine nuts. Good any time of day.

1½ cups all-purpose flour
3 tablespoons granulated sugar
1 teaspoon baking powder
¼ teaspoon salt
½ cup unsalted butter, chilled
1 large egg

1 tablespoon milk
½ teaspoon vanilla extract
½ cup raisins
1 egg yolk mixed with ½ teaspoon water
  for glaze
3 tablespoons pine nuts or slivered almonds

Preheat oven to 375°F. Lightly butter a baking sheet.

In a large bowl, stir together the flour, sugar, baking powder, and salt. Cut the butter into ½-inch cubes and distribute them over the flour mixture. With a pastry blender or two knives used scissors fashion, cut in the butter until the mixture resembles coarse crumbs. In a small bowl, stir together the egg, milk, and vanilla. Add the milk mixture to the flour mixture and stir to combine. Stir in the raisins. With lightly floured hands, divide the dough into 6 equal-sized pieces (about ⅓ cup each). Shape into balls and press into 2½-inch-diameter circles on the prepared baking sheet, leaving about 3 inches between scones. Brush the top and sides with the egg mixture and top each with ½ tablespoon pine nuts. Press nuts lightly into the dough. Bake for 20 to 25 minutes, or until a cake tester or toothpick inserted into the center of a scone comes out clean.

Remove the baking sheet to a wire rack and cool for 5 minutes. Using a spatula, transfer the scones to the wire rack to cool. Serve warm, or cool completely and store in an airtight container.

Makes 6 scones

• SPICED WHOLE-WHEAT SCONES •

A hint of spice in these whole-wheat scones makes them especially nice. They are lovely with many of the fruit spreads.

1 cup whole-wheat flour
1 cup all-purpose flour
⅓ cup granulated sugar
1½ teaspoons baking powder
½ teaspoon baking soda
½ teaspoon ground cinnamon
¼ teaspoon salt
⅛ teaspoon ground ginger

Pinch ground nutmeg
Pinch ground cloves
6 tablespoons unsalted butter, chilled
½ cup buttermilk
1 large egg
1 teaspoon vanilla extract
⅔ cup raisins (optional)

Preheat oven to 400°F. Lightly butter a 9-inch-diameter circle in the center of a baking sheet.

In a large bowl, stir together the flours, sugar, baking powder, baking soda, cinnamon, salt, ginger, nutmeg, and cloves. Cut the butter into ½-inch cubes and distribute them over the flour mixture. With a pastry blender or two knives used scissors fashion, cut in the butter until the mixture resembles coarse crumbs. In a small bowl, stir together the buttermilk, egg, and vanilla. Add the buttermilk mixture to the flour mixture and stir to combine. Stir in the raisins, if desired.

With lightly floured hands, pat the dough into an 8-inch-diameter circle in the center of the prepared baking sheet. With a serrated knife, cut into 8 wedges. Bake for

16 to 18 minutes, or until the top is lightly browned and a cake tester or toothpick inserted into the center of a scone comes out clean.

Remove the baking sheet to a wire rack and cool for 5 minutes. Using a spatula, transfer the scones to the wire rack to cool. Recut into wedges, if necessary. Serve warm, or cool completely and store in an airtight container.

Makes 8 scones

• STREUSEL SCONES •

A cakelike scone with a hint of pineapple, filled and topped with a pecan coconut streusel.

STREUSEL TOPPING/FILLING

1/3 cup all-purpose flour	3 tablespoons unsalted butter, chilled
1/3 cup firmly packed light brown sugar	1/2 cup finely chopped walnuts
1/4 teaspoon ground cinnamon	1/4 cup shredded coconut

SCONE

2 cups all-purpose flour	1/3 cup unsalted butter, chilled
1/3 cup granulated sugar	1/2 cup crushed pineapple in juice,
2 teaspoons baking powder	undrained, (1/2 of an 8-ounce can)
1/8 teaspoon baking soda	1 large egg
1/2 teaspoon salt	1 teaspoon vanilla extract

Preheat oven to 375°F. Lightly butter a 10-inch-diameter circle in the center of a baking sheet.

To prepare streusel:
In a small bowl, stir together the flour, brown sugar, and cinnamon. Cut the butter into 1/2-inch cubes and distribute them over the flour mixture. With a pastry blender or two knives used scissors fashion, cut in the butter until the mixture resembles coarse crumbs. Stir in the walnuts and coconut. Set aside.

To prepare the scones:

In a large bowl, stir together the flour, sugar, baking powder, baking soda, and salt. Cut the butter into ½-inch cubes and distribute them over the flour mixture. With a pastry blender or two knives used scissors fashion, cut in the butter until the mixture resembles coarse crumbs. In a small bowl, stir together the pineapple, egg, and vanilla. Add the pineapple mixture to the flour mixture and stir to combine. The dough will be slightly sticky.

With lightly floured hands, pat half of the dough into an 8-inch-diameter circle in the center of the prepared baking sheet. Reserving ⅔ cup of the streusel for topping, sprinkle the remaining streusel on the dough to within one inch of the edges. Press down lightly. With lightly floured hands, pat the dough into an 8-inch-diameter circle on a lightly floured cutting board. Place the dough over the streusel-topped dough on the baking sheet.

Press the edges to seal well. Sprinkle the top with the remaining ⅔ cup of streusel. Press lightly. Bake 25 to 35 minutes, or until a cake tester or toothpick inserted in the center comes out clean. Remove the baking sheet to a wire rack and cool for 15 minutes. With a spatula, transfer the scones to the wire rack to cool. When ready to serve, cut into 8 wedges. Serve warm, or cool completely and store in an airtight container.

Makes 8 scones

• TRIPLE CHOCOLATE CHUNK SCONES •

These tender scones are studded with chunks of bittersweet, milk, and white chocolate. Our dropped scones are great any time of day. Served with a glass of milk, they make a welcomed after-school snack.

2 cups all-purpose flour
1/3 cup firmly packed dark brown sugar
1 1/2 teaspoons baking powder
1/4 teaspoon baking soda
1/4 teaspoon salt
1/4 cup unsalted butter, chilled
1/2 cup buttermilk
1 large egg

1 1/2 teaspoons vanilla extract
3 ounces bittersweet chocolate, cut into 1/2-inch pieces
3 ounces milk chocolate, cut into 1/2-inch pieces
3 ounces white chocolate, cut into 1/2-inch pieces

Preheat oven to 375°F.

In a large bowl, stir together the flour, brown sugar, baking powder, baking soda, and salt. Cut the butter into 1/2-inch cubes and distribute them over the flour mixture. With a pastry blender or two knives used scissors fashion, cut in the butter until the mixture resembles coarse crumbs. In a small bowl, stir together the buttermilk, egg, and vanilla. Add the buttermilk mixture to the flour mixture and stir to combine. Stir in the chocolate chunks until they are evenly distributed.

Using a 1/4-cup measuring cup, drop the dough onto an ungreased baking sheet, leaving about 2 inches between scones. Bake for 23 to 25 minutes, or until the tops are lightly browned and a cake tester or toothpick inserted into the center of a scone comes out clean.

Remove the baking sheet to a wire rack and cool for 5 minutes. Using a spatula, transfer the scones to the wire rack to cool. Serve warm, or cool completely and store in an airtight container.

These scones freeze well.

Makes approximately 10 scones

• TROPICAL SCONES •

One bite of these fruity, nutty scones will take you on a trip to the islands. These sweet treats provide a summery addition at any time of the year.

2 cups all-purpose flour
1/4 cup granulated sugar
2 teaspoons baking powder
1/4 teaspoon salt
5 tablespoons unsalted butter, chilled
1/2 cup milk
1 large egg

1 1/2 teaspoons vanilla extract
1/2 cup chopped dried papaya
1/2 cup chopped dried pineapple
1/2 cup chopped macadamia nuts
1/2 cup shredded coconut
3 ounces white chocolate, cut into 1/2-inch pieces

Preheat oven to 375°F. Lightly butter a 9-inch-diameter circle in the center of a baking sheet.

In a large bowl, stir together the flour, sugar, baking powder, and salt. Cut the butter into 1/2-inch cubes and distribute them over the flour mixture. With a pastry blender or two knives used scissors fashion, cut in the butter until the mixture resembles coarse crumbs. In a small bowl, stir together the milk, egg, and vanilla. Add the milk mixture to the flour mixture and stir to combine. Stir in the papaya, pineapple, macadamia nuts, coconut, and white chocolate until evenly distributed.

With lightly floured hands, pat the dough into a 8-inch-diameter circle in the center of the prepared baking sheet. With a serrated knife, cut into 8 wedges. Bake for 18 to 20 minutes, or until the top is lightly browned and a cake tester or toothpick inserted into the center of a scone comes out clean.

Remove the baking sheet to a wire rack and cool for 5 minutes. Using a spatula, transfer the scones to the wire rack to cool. Recut into wedges, if necessary. Serve warm, or cool completely and store in an airtight container.

These scones freeze well.

Makes 8 scones

• TWO-TONE SCONES •

Two-layered jumbo-sized scones. This scone combines two of America's favorite muffin flavors. Making this scone can be easily divided between two people.

One recipe of Corn Scones dough (page 36)
One recipe of Bran Scones dough (page 22)

Preheat oven to 375°F. Lightly butter an 11-inch-diameter circle in the center of a baking sheet.

With lightly floured hands, pat the Corn Scone dough into a 9-inch-diameter circle in the center of the prepared baking sheet. With lightly floured hands, form the Bran Scone dough into a disk and pat it onto the top of the Corn Scone circle. The Bran Scone circle should be about 8 inches in diameter. With a serrated knife, cut into 8 wedges. Bake for 22 to 24 minutes, or until the top is lightly browned and a cake tester or toothpick inserted into the center of a scone comes out clean.

Remove the baking sheet to a wire rack and cool for 5 minutes. Using a spatula, transfer the scones to the wire rack to cool. Recut into wedges, if necessary. Serve warm, or cool completely and store in an airtight container.

Makes 8 jumbo scones

Savory Scones

• CALZONE SCONES •

These are much easier to make than the classic yeast calzones. Try them with a bowl of soup for a light lunch or dinner.

2 cups all-purpose flour
½ cup grated Parmesan cheese, divided
2 teaspoons baking powder
¼ teaspoon dried leaf basil, crumbled
¼ teaspoon dried leaf oregano, crumbled
¼ teaspoon salt
⅛ teaspoon plus a generous pinch ground black pepper

6 tablespoons unsalted butter, chilled
⅓ cup milk
1 large egg
⅓ cup shredded mozzarella cheese
¼ cup ricotta cheese
¼ cup thawed and well-drained chopped spinach (see Note)
1 egg, lightly beaten for glaze

Preheat oven to 400°F.

In a large bowl, stir together the flour, ¼ cup of the Parmesan cheese, baking powder, basil, oregano, salt, and ⅛ teaspoon pepper. Cut the butter into ½-inch cubes and distribute them over the flour mixture. With a pastry blender or two knives used scissors fashion, cut in the butter until the mixture resembles coarse crumbs. In a small bowl, stir together the milk and egg. Stir the milk mixture into the flour mixture and knead until combined.

In a medium bowl, stir together the mozzarella, ricotta, the remaining ¼ cup of the Parmesan, the spinach, and the generous dash of pepper.

With lightly floured hands, pat the dough into a ¼-inch thickness on a lightly floured cutting board. Using a 2½- to 3-inch-diameter crinkled round biscuit cutter, cut out rounds from the dough. Gather the scraps together and repeat until there are 18 rounds. Place 9 of the rounds on an ungreased baking sheet. Top each round with 1 tablespoon of the spinach/cheese mixture. Lightly brush the edges of these 9 circles with the egg mixture and top each round with one of the remaining circles of dough. Press the edges gently to seal. Lightly brush the tops with the egg. Bake for 15 to 17 minutes, or until lightly browned.

Remove the baking sheet to a wire rack and cool for 5 minutes. Using a spatula, transfer the scones to the wire rack to cool. These scones are best served warm.

Makes 9 scones

Note: Squeeze the thawed spinach in paper towels or a clean dish towel to remove moisture.

• CHEESE SCONES •

Parmesan and Cheddar flavor these delicious scones. A warm cheese scone and a bowl of hearty beef stew on a cold and wintery day is sure to chase the chills away.

2 cups all-purpose flour
2 teaspoons baking powder
¼ teaspoon salt
Generous dash ground red pepper
1½ cups shredded Cheddar cheese
3 tablespoons grated Parmesan cheese

⅓ cup unsalted butter, chilled
⅓ cup milk
2 large eggs
1 egg yolk mixed with 1 teaspoon water for glaze (optional)

Preheat oven to 400°F. Lightly butter a 10-inch-diameter circle in the center of a baking sheet.

In a large bowl, stir together the flour, baking powder, salt, and red pepper. Stir in the cheeses. Cut the butter into ½-inch cubes and distribute them over the flour mixture. With a pastry blender or two knives used scissors fashion, cut in the butter until the mixture resembles coarse crumbs. In a small bowl, stir together the milk and 2 eggs. Add the milk mixture to the flour mixture and stir until combined.

Spread the dough into an 8-inch-diameter circle in the center of the prepared baking sheet. If desired, brush the egg mixture over the top of the dough. With a serrated knife, cut into 8 wedges. Bake for 15 to 17 minutes, or until the top is lightly browned and a cake tester or toothpick inserted into the center of a scone comes out clean.

Remove the baking sheet to a wire rack and cool for 5 minutes. Using a spatula, transfer the scones to the wire rack to cool. Recut into wedges, if necessary. Serve warm, or cool completely and store in an airtight container in the refrigerator. Let the scones reach room temperature before serving.

Makes 8 scones

• DILLED SCALLION SCONES •

Delicious served warm with cream cheese.

1½ cups all-purpose flour	*½ cup sliced scallion*
½ cup whole wheat flour	*2 tablespoons chopped fresh dill weed*
2 teaspoons baking powder	*¼ cup unsalted butter, chilled*
½ teaspoon baking soda	*⅓ cup buttermilk*
½ teaspoon salt	*1 large egg*

Preheat oven to 400°F. Lightly butter a 9-inch-diameter circle in the center of a baking sheet.

In a large bowl, stir together the flours, baking powder, baking soda, and salt. Stir in the scallion and dill weed. Cut the butter into ½-inch cubes and distribute them over the flour mixture. With a pastry blender or two knives used scissors fashion, cut in the butter until incorporated into the mixture. In a small bowl, stir together the buttermilk and egg. Add the buttermilk mixture to the flour mixture and knead together until combined.

With lightly floured hands, pat the dough into a 7-inch-diameter circle in the center of the prepared baking sheet. With a serrated knife, cut into 8 wedges. Bake for 15 to 17 minutes, or until a toothpick inserted into the center of a scone comes out clean.

Remove the baking sheet to a wire rack and cool for 5 minutes. Using a spatula, transfer the scones to the wire rack to cool. Recut into wedges, if necessary. Serve warm or cool completely and store in an airtight container.

Makes 8 scones

• HEARTY GRAIN SCONES •

These scones are packed with an assortment of grains.

½ cup buttermilk
1 large egg
1 tablespoon molasses
1 tablespoon honey
¼ cup unprocessed bran
½ cup all-purpose flour
½ cup whole-wheat flour
¼ cup rye flour

¼ cup plus 1½ tablespoons uncooked old-
   fashioned rolled oats
¼ cup yellow cornmeal
2 teaspoons baking powder
½ teaspoon baking soda
½ teaspoon salt
6 tablespoons unsalted butter, chilled

Preheat oven to 400°F. Lightly butter a 9-inch-diameter circle in the center of a baking sheet.

In a small bowl, stir together the buttermilk, egg, molasses, and honey. Stir in the bran and let stand for at least 2 minutes, or until the cereal is softened. In a large bowl, stir together the flours, ¼ cup of the oats, cornmeal, baking powder, baking soda, and salt. Cut the butter into ½-inch cubes and distribute them over the flour mixture. With a pastry blender or two knives used scissors fashion, cut in the butter until the mixture resembles coarse crumbs. Add the bran mixture to the flour mixture and stir to combine.

With lightly floured hands, pat the dough into an 8-inch-diameter circle in the center of the prepared baking sheet. Sprinkle the surface of the dough evenly with the remaining 1½ tablespoons of oatmeal. With a serrated knife, cut into 8 wedges. Bake for 16 to 18 minutes, or until the top is lightly browned and a cake tester or toothpick inserted into the center of a scone comes out clean.

Remove the baking sheet to a wire rack and cool for 5 minutes. Using a spatula, transfer the scones to the wire rack to cool. Recut into wedges, if necessary. Serve warm, or cool completely and store in an airtight container.

Makes 8 scones

• IRISH SODA BREAD SCONES •

These mildly sweet scones are perfect at meals or snacktime. Don't forget to serve them on St. Patrick's Day.

2 cups all-purpose flour
3 tablespoons firmly packed light brown sugar
1½ teaspoons baking powder
½ teaspoon baking soda
½ teaspoon caraway seeds
½ teaspoon salt
⅓ cup unsalted butter, chilled

½ cup buttermilk
1 large egg
½ cup coarsely chopped walnuts
¼ cup raisins
¼ cup golden raisins (see Note)
1 egg yolk mixed with ½ teaspoon water for glaze (optional)

Preheat oven to 375°F. Butter a 10-inch-diameter circle in the center of a baking sheet.

In a large bowl, stir together the flour, brown sugar, baking powder, baking soda, caraway seeds, and salt. Cut the butter into ½-inch cubes and distribute them over the flour mixture. With a pastry blender or two knives used scissors fashion, cut in the butter until the mixture resembles coarse crumbs. In a small bowl, stir together the buttermilk and egg. Add the buttermilk mixture to the flour mixture and stir to combine. The dough will be sticky. With lightly floured hands, knead in the nuts and raisins until evenly distributed.

With lightly floured hands, pat the dough into a 9-inch-diameter circle in the center of the prepared baking sheet. If desired, brush the egg mixture over the top and sides of the dough. With a serrated knife, cut into 8 wedges. Bake for 20 to 25 minutes, or until a cake tester or toothpick inserted into the center of a scone comes out clean.

Remove the baking sheet to a wire rack to cool for 10 minutes. Using a spatula, transfer the scones to the wire rack to cool. Recut into wedges, if necessary. Serve warm or cool completely and store in an airtight container.

These scones freeze well.

Makes 8 scones

Note: ½ cup dark or golden raisins may be used instead of two varieties.

• PESTO CHEESE SCONES •

Perfect served with minestrone soup or an Italian dinner.

2 cups all-purpose flour
2 tablespoons grated Parmesan cheese
2 teaspoons baking powder
1/4 teaspoon salt
1/3 cup unsalted butter, chilled
1/4 cup pine nuts or walnuts, divided
1/2 cup fresh basil leaves

1 tablespoon olive oil
1/2 small garlic clove, minced
1 large egg
2 tablespoons milk
1/2 cup shredded Provolone cheese
1 egg white mixed with 1/2 teaspoon water
for glaze

Preheat oven to 375°F. Butter a 9-inch-diameter circle in the center of a baking sheet.

In a large bowl, stir together the flour, Parmesan cheese, baking powder, and salt. Cut the butter into 1/2-inch cubes and distribute them over the flour mixture. With a pastry blender or two knives used scissors fashion, cut in the butter until the mixture resembles coarse crumbs.

Place 1 tablespoon of the pine nuts in the container of a food processor fitted with a steel blade. Process until finely chopped. Scrape nuts into a small bowl. Add the basil, oil, and garlic to the container of the food processor. Process for 20 seconds or until the basil is finely chopped, stopping to scrape down the sides of the container with a rubber scraper, if necessary. Scrape the mixture into the small bowl. Stir the egg and milk into the basil mixture. Add the basil mixture to the flour mixture and stir to combine. The dough will be sticky. With lightly floured hands, knead in the Provolone cheese until evenly distributed. With lightly floured hands, pat the dough into an 8-inch-diameter circle in the center of the prepared baking sheet.

Brush the egg mixture over the top and sides of the dough. With a serrated knife, cut into 8 wedges. Sprinkle the surface of the dough with the remaining 3 tablespoons of pine nuts and press them gently into the dough. Bake for 25 to 30 minutes, or until a cake tester or toothpick inserted into the center of a scone comes out clean.

Remove the baking sheet to a wire rack and cool for 5 minutes. Using a spatula, transfer the scones to the wire rack to cool. Recut into wedges, if necessary. Serve warm, or cool completely and store in an airtight container in the refrigerator.

Makes 8 scones

• POTATO BACON SCONES •

These scones provide a wonderful use for leftover cooked potatoes. Try these scones for breakfast.

5 strips of bacon
1 cup mashed cooked potatoes
1 large egg

¼ teaspoon salt
⅛ teaspoon ground black pepper
¼ cup all-purpose flour

In a large skillet, cook the bacon over medium heat until it is crispy. Using a slotted spoon, remove the strips of bacon to paper towels to drain. Pour out and reserve the drippings. Cool and chop the bacon into ¼-inch pieces.

In a medium bowl, beat together the potatoes, egg, salt, and pepper until combined. Beat in two tablespoons of the reserved bacon drippings. Beat in the flour until combined. Stir in the chopped bacon.

In the same skillet, heat 1 tablespoon of the reserved drippings over medium high heat. Using a ¼-cup measuring cup, drop the potato mixture onto the hot skillet. Cook for 3 to 4 minutes on each side, or until the scones are golden brown on both sides. Add additional bacon drippings as necessary. Drain the scones on paper towels. Serve warm.

Makes approximately 7 scones

• RYE CARAWAY SCONES •

Split these scones and fill them with ham, cheese, and mustard for mini sandwiches.

1 cup all-purpose flour	*½ teaspoon baking soda*
¾ cup rye flour	*¼ teaspoon salt*
2 tablespoons granulated sugar	*⅓ cup unsalted butter, chilled*
2½ teaspoons baking powder	*⅔ cup buttermilk*
2 teaspoons caraway seeds	*½ cup currants (optional)*

Preheat oven to 400°F. Lightly butter a baking sheet.

In a large bowl, stir together the flours, sugar, baking powder, caraway seeds, baking soda, and salt. Cut the butter into ½-inch cubes and distribute them over the flour mixture. With a pastry blender or two knives used scissors fashion, cut in the butter until the mixture resembles coarse crumbs. Stir the buttermilk into the flour mixture and knead until combined. Knead in the currants, if desired.

With lightly floured hands, pat the dough into a ½-inch thickness on a lightly floured cutting board. Using a 2½-inch-diameter round biscuit cutter or glass, cut out rounds from the dough. Gather the scraps together and repeat until all the dough is used. Place the rounds on the prepared baking sheet and bake for 15 to 17 minutes, or until lightly browned.

Remove the baking sheet to a wire rack and cool for 5 minutes. Using a spatula, transfer the scones to the wire rack to cool. Serve warm, or cool completely and store in an airtight container.

Makes approximately 10 scones

• SCONE-CRUSTED PIZZA •

Beer knows no better partner! For including this recipe in a book on scones, we owe the British a royal apology—we're sure they thought they'd never top anything related to a scone with artichoke hearts, roasted red peppers, goat cheese, and olives. We'd like to think that this recipe is an example of "American ingenuity." Whatever it represents, this pizza makes a wonderful light lunch or supper. Try topping the scone base with other "pizza" ingredients for hassle-free homemade pizza.

1 cup whole-wheat flour
1/2 cup all-purpose flour
3 tablespoons finely chopped walnuts
1 1/2 teaspoons baking powder
1/8 teaspoon salt
1/4 cup unsalted butter, chilled
1/4 cup milk
1 large egg
One jar (6 ounces) marinated artichoke
    hearts

1/2 teaspoon dried leaf basil, crumbled
1/4 teaspoon dried leaf oregano, crumbled
1/2 cup chopped roasted red peppers
1/3 cup chopped pitted oil-cured olives or
    ripe olives
5 ounces goat cheese, cut into 1/2-inch pieces
8 ounces shredded mozzarella cheese

Preheat oven to 400°F. Lightly butter an 11-inch-diameter circle in the center of a baking sheet.

In a large bowl, stir together the flours, walnuts, baking powder, and salt. Cut the butter into 1/2-inch cubes and distribute them over the flour mixture. With a pastry blender or two knives used scissors fashion, cut in the butter until the mixture resembles coarse crumbs. In a small bowl, stir together the milk and egg. Add the milk mixture to the flour mixture and stir to combine.

With lightly floured hands, pat the dough into a 10-inch-diameter circle in the center of the prepared baking sheet.

Reserving 1 tablespoon of the marinade, drain the artichokes (leftover marinade can be added to salad dressings). Cut the artichoke hearts into quarters. Brush the surface of the dough with the reserved tablespoon of marinade and sprinkle it with the basil and oregano.

Evenly distribute the artichokes, red peppers, olives, and goat cheese over the surface. Top with the mozzarella cheese. Bake for 23 to 25 minutes, or until the cheese is melted and the crust is lightly browned.

Remove the baking sheet to a wire rack. Cool slightly and cut into 8 to 10 wedges.
Makes 8 to 10 slices of pizza

The mildly spicy scone flecked with Cheddar cheese and chilies is perfect with Taco Spread (page 112) and a bowl of chili.

1½ cups all-purpose flour
½ cup yellow cornmeal
1 tablespoon granulated sugar
2 teaspoons baking powder
¼ teaspoon salt
¼ teaspoon chili powder
⅛ teaspoon ground cumin
⅛ teaspoon ground black pepper (optional)
⅓ cup unsalted butter, chilled

1 large egg
3 tablespoons milk
3 tablespoons undrained chopped, canned green chilies
½ cup (about 2 ounces) shredded sharp Cheddar cheese
1 egg yolk mixed with ½ teaspoon water for glaze

Preheat oven to 375°F. Lightly butter a 9-inch-diameter circle in the center of a baking sheet.

In a large bowl, stir together the flour, cornmeal, sugar, baking powder, salt, chili powder, cumin, and pepper, if desired. Cut the butter into ½-inch cubes and distribute them over the flour mixture. With a pastry blender or two knives used scissors fashion, cut in the butter until the mixture resembles coarse crumbs. In a small bowl, stir together the egg, milk, and chilies. Add the egg mixture to the flour mixture and stir to combine. The dough will be sticky. With lightly floured hands, knead in the cheese until evenly distributed.

With lightly floured hands, pat the dough into an 8-inch-diameter circle in the center of the prepared baking sheet. Brush the egg mixture over the top and sides of the dough. With a serrated knife, cut into 8 wedges. Bake for 20 to 25 minutes, or until the top is lightly browned and a cake tester or toothpick inserted into the center of a scone comes out clean.

Remove the baking sheet to a wire rack and cool for 5 minutes. Using a spatula, transfer the scones to the wire rack to cool. Recut into wedges, if necessary. Serve warm, or cool completely and store in an airtight container in the refrigerator.

Makes 8 scones

• WHOLE-WHEAT SCONES •

Reminiscent of Scottish wheat-meal scones, these mildly flavored scones go well with a variety of spreads.

⅔ cup all-purpose flour
⅔ cup whole-wheat flour
2 tablespoons granulated sugar
1 teaspoon cream of tartar
½ teaspoon baking soda
¼ teaspoon salt
¼ cup unsalted butter, chilled

¼ cup milk
½ teaspoon milk for glaze (optional)
1 teaspoon granulated sugar for glaze
  (optional)
Generous dash ground cinnamon for glaze
  (optional)

Preheat oven to 375°F. Lightly butter a baking sheet.

In a large bowl, stir together the flours, sugar, cream of tartar, baking soda, and salt. Cut the butter into ½-inch cubes and distribute them over the flour mixture. With a pastry blender or two knives used scissors fashion, cut in the butter until the mixture resembles coarse crumbs. Add the milk to the flour mixture and stir to combine. The dough will be slightly sticky.

With lightly floured hands, divide the dough into 4 equal-sized pieces (about ⅓ cup each). Shape into balls and press into 3-inch-diameter circles on the prepared baking sheet, leaving about 3 inches between scones. Brush the tops and sides with the ½ teaspoon of milk, if desired. Combine the sugar and cinnamon and sprinkle the mixture over the tops of the scones, if desired. Bake for 18 to 20 minutes, or until a cake tester or toothpick inserted into the center of a scone comes out clean.

Remove the baking sheet to a wire rack and cool for 5 minutes. Using a spatula, transfer the scones to the wire rack to cool. Serve warm, or cool completely and store in an airtight container.

Makes 4 scones

• UPTOWN SCONES •

Pieces of sun-dried tomatoes, pine nuts, and Reggiano Parmesan cheese "yuppify" these savory scone wedges. These scones are perfect with soups and/or salads.

2 cups all-purpose flour
½ cup grated Parmesan cheese, preferably Reggiano
2 teaspoons baking powder
1 teaspoon dried basil leaves, crumbled
¼ teaspoon salt
¼ cup unsalted butter, chilled

⅓ cup milk
2 large eggs
¼ teaspoon hot pepper sauce
¾ cup coarsely chopped, drained sun-dried tomatoes (packed in olive oil)
½ cup plus 2 tablespoons pine nuts

Preheat oven to 400°F. Lightly butter a 10-inch-diameter circle in the center of a baking sheet.

In a large bowl, stir together the flour, cheese, baking powder, basil, and salt. Cut the butter into ½-inch cubes and distribute them over the flour mixture. With a pastry blender or two knives used scissors fashion, cut in the butter until the mixture resembles coarse crumbs. In a small bowl, stir together the milk, eggs, and hot pepper sauce. Add the milk mixture to the flour mixture and stir to combine. Stir in the tomatoes and ½ cup of the pine nuts. The dough will be sticky.

With lightly floured hands, pat the dough into a 9-inch-diameter circle in the center of the prepared baking sheet. Sprinkle the surface of the dough with the remaining two tablespoons of pine nuts and press them gently into the dough. With a serrated knife, cut into 8 wedges. Bake for 20 to 25 minutes, or until the top is lightly browned and a cake tester or toothpick inserted into the center of a scone comes out clean.

Remove the baking sheet to a wire rack and cool for 5 minutes. Using a spatula, transfer the scones to the wire rack to cool. Recut into wedges, if necessary. Serve warm or cool completely and store in an airtight container in the refrigerator. Let the scones reach room temperature or warm slightly before serving.

These scones freeze well.

Makes 8 scones

Spreads

◆ A SIMPLY SPIRITED SPREAD ◆

6 ounces cream cheese, softened
⅓ cup chopped pitted dates
¼ cup chopped walnuts

2 teaspoons rum
1 teaspoon firmly packed dark brown sugar

Place the cream cheese, dates, nuts, rum, and brown sugar in the container of a food processor fitted with a steel blade. Process for 45 seconds, or until almost smooth, stopping to scrape down the sides of the container, if necessary.

Scrape the spread into a small bowl. Serve immediately or cover and refrigerate. To serve, let stand for 10 minutes at room temperature to soften.

Makes approximately 1 cup

◆ APPLE BUTTER SPREAD ◆

4 ounces cream cheese, softened
¼ cup apple butter

¼ teaspoon vanilla extract
Dash ground cinnamon

Place the cream cheese, apple butter, vanilla, and cinnamon in the container of a food processor fitted with a steel blade. Process for 20 seconds, or just until smooth, stopping to scrape down the sides of the container, if necessary.

Scrape the spread into a small bowl. Cover and refrigerate until slightly firm.

Makes approximately ⅔ cup

◆ CHOCOLATE CREAM CHEESE ◆

3 tablespoons unsalted butter
1 ounce bittersweet chocolate
3 ounces cream cheese, softened

¼ cup confectioners' sugar
¼ teaspoon vanilla extract
2 tablespoons sour cream

In the top of a double boiler, over hot, not simmering, water, melt the butter and chocolate, stirring often. Remove the pan from the heat and cool for 5 minutes. In a small bowl, with a fork, beat the cream cheese until smooth. Beat in the sugar and vanilla. Gradually beat in the chocolate mixture until blended. Stir in the sour cream.

Cover and refrigerate until slightly firm. To serve, let stand for 5 minutes at room temperature to soften.

Makes approximately ⅞ cup

◆ CHOCOLATE NUT BUTTER ◆

1 bar (4 ounces) sweet baking chocolate,
  coarsely broken

⅓ cup smooth peanut butter

In the top of a double boiler, over hot, not simmering, water, melt the chocolate. Remove the pan from the heat and stir in the peanut butter. Let stand at room temperature or cover and refrigerate until slightly firm.

Makes approximately ⅔ cup

• CHUTNEY CREAM CHEESE SPREAD •

4 ounces cream cheese, softened
3 tablespoons finely chopped Major Grey's
   chutney

3 tablespoons finely chopped walnuts

In a small bowl, stir together the cream cheese, chutney, and walnuts until combined.
   Serve spread immediately or cover and refrigerate. To serve, let stand for 15 minutes at room temperature to soften.
   Makes approximately ⅔ cup

• CITRUS BUTTER •

½ cup unsalted butter, softened
1½ tablespoons confectioners' sugar
¼ teaspoon grated lemon peel

¼ teaspoon grated lime peel
¼ teaspoon grated orange peel

In a small bowl, stir together the butter, sugar, and lemon, lime, and orange peels until combined.
   Serve the butter immediately or cover and refrigerate. To serve, let stand for 15 minutes at room temperature to soften.
   Makes approximately ½ cup

• CITRUS CURD •

2 large eggs plus 2 large egg yolks
¾ cup granulated sugar
⅓ cup freshly squeezed lemon juice
⅓ cup freshly squeezed orange juice

1 teaspoon grated lemon peel
1 teaspoon grated orange peel
Few grains of salt
⅓ cup unsalted butter, chilled

In a heavy-bottomed medium saucepan, whisk together the eggs and yolks to combine. Whisk in the sugar, lemon juice, orange juice, lemon peel, orange peel, and salt. Cut the butter into ½-inch cubes and add to the saucepan. Stirring constantly, cook the mixture just until it comes to a boil and thickens. Do not overcook as it will curdle. Pour the mixture into a heatproof glass container. Cover the surface with plastic wrap and refrigerate.

Makes approximately 2 cups

• CLOTTED CREAM •

Clotted cream is best made if you are in England and have a cow standing nearby. A good American substitute can be made by beating heavy cream until it is very stiff. For more authenticity, use Devon cream, which is occasionally available in the United States. Believe it or not, controversy exists as to which comes first when you're topping a scone: the jam/preserves or the clotted cream. We believe that this is a matter of personal preference—smear them on in any order you want!

• CREAMY CRANBERRY SPREAD •

3 ounces cream cheese, softened   *3 tablespoons cranberry orange sauce*

In a small bowl, stir together the cream cheese and cranberry orange sauce until combined.

Serve the spread immediately or cover and refrigerate. To serve, let stand for 15 minutes to soften.

Makes approximately ½ cup

• CREAMY STRAWBERRY SPREAD •

1 package (7½ ounces) farmer cheese
1 cup sliced strawberries
2 tablespoons confectioners sugar

1 teaspoon orange-flavored liqueur
  (optional)
¼ teaspoon vanilla extract

Place the cheese, strawberries, sugar, liqueur (if desired), and vanilla in the container of a food processor fitted with a steel blade. Process for 15 seconds, or just until smooth, stopping to scrape down the sides of the container, if necessary. Do not overprocess or mixture will be very thin.

Scrape the spread into a small bowl. Serve immediately or cover and refrigerate.

Makes approximately 1⅓ cups

• CREAMY PEANUT BUTTER RAISIN SPREAD •

3 ounces cream cheese, softened
2 tablespoons smooth peanut butter
2 tablespoons chopped raisins

1 teaspoon firmly packed light brown sugar
½ teaspoon vanilla extract

In a small bowl, stir together the cream cheese, peanut butter, raisins, brown sugar, and vanilla until combined.

Serve the spread immediately or cover and refrigerate. To serve, let stand for 15 minutes at room temperature to soften.

Makes approximately ½ cup

• DILLED SALMON CREAM CHEESE SPREAD •

Try this with Dilled Scallion or Hearty Grain Scones.

3 ounces cream cheese, softened
¼ cup chopped smoked salmon
1 teaspoon fresh dill or ¼ teaspoon dried
  dill weed

Generous dash freshly ground black pepper

In a small bowl, stir together the cream cheese, salmon, dill, and pepper until combined. Serve the spread immediately or cover and refrigerate. To serve, let stand for 15 minutes at room temperature to soften.

Makes approximately ½ cup

• MAPLE BUTTER •

¼ *cup unsalted butter, softened*
2 *teaspoons maple syrup*

1 to 2 drops maple extract (optional)

In a small bowl, stir together the butter, maple syrup, and maple extract, if desired, until combined.

Serve the butter immediately or cover and refrigerate. To serve, let stand for 15 minutes at room temperature to soften.

Makes approximately ¼ cup

• PISTACHIO HONEY SPREAD •

⅓ *cup unsalted shelled pistachio nuts*
4 *ounces cream cheese, softened*
2 *teaspoons honey*

2 *teaspoons lime juice*
Chopped shelled pistachio nuts for garnish
  (optional)

Place the nuts in the container of a food processor fitted with a steel blade. Process just until the nuts are finely chopped. Add the cream cheese, honey, and lime juice. Process for 15 seconds, or just until smooth, stopping to scrape down the sides of the container, if necessary.

Scrape the spread into a small bowl. Garnish with the additional chopped nuts, if desired. Serve immediately or cover and refrigerate. To serve, let stand for 10 minutes at room temperature to soften.

Makes approximately ¾ cup

• RASPBERRY CREAM CHEESE •

3 ounces cream cheese, softened   *1½ tablespoons raspberry preserves*

In a small bowl, stir together the cream cheese and the raspberry preserves until combined.

Serve the spread immediately or cover and refrigerate. To serve, let stand for 15 minutes at room temperature to soften.

Makes approximately scant ½ cup

• TACO SPREAD •

4 ounces cream cheese, softened   *⅛ teaspoon granulated sugar*
2 tablespoons undrained chopped, canned   *⅛ teaspoon chili powder*
* green chilies*   *Generous dash ground cumin*
2 tablespoons mild taco sauce

Place the cream cheese, chilies, taco sauce, sugar, chili powder, and cumin in the container of a food processor fitted with a steel blade. Process for 20 seconds or until smooth, stopping to scrape down the sides of the container, if necessary.

Scrape the spread into a small bowl. Serve immediately at room temperature or cover and refrigerate.

Makes approximately ¾ cup

• WHITE CHOCOLATE CREAM CHEESE •

3 ounces white chocolate or white chocolate
   with nougat pieces
1 tablespoon unsalted butter
4 ounces cream cheese, softened

1 teaspoon cognac or brandy
¼ teaspoon vanilla extract
2 tablespoons sour cream

In the top of a double boiler over hot, not simmering, water, melt the chocolate and butter, stirring often. Stir in the cream cheese until combined. Add the cognac and vanilla and stir until smooth. Remove the pan from the heat and cool slightly. Stir in the sour cream.

Scrape the mixture into a small bowl. Cover and refrigerate until slightly firm. To serve, let stand for 10 minutes at room temperature to soften.

Makes approximately ⅞ cup

◆ YOGURT CHEESE ◆

Yogurt cheese can be flavored in a variety of ways. A couple suggestions follow.

PLAIN YOGURT CHEESE
1 container (32 ounces) plain yogurt

Line a colander or strainer with cheesecloth or a clean dish towel. Place the colander in the sink or over a bowl. Spoon the yogurt into the center of the colander and gather up the edges of the towel. Drain the yogurt overnight or for at least 6 hours at room temperature; the longer the yogurt drains, the firmer the finished cheese will be.
   Makes approximately 1 cup cheese

CINNAMON-DATE YOGURT CHEESE
1 recipe of Plain Yogurt Cheese　　　　　*1 tablespoon granulated sugar*
⅓ cup finely chopped pitted dates　　　*¼ teaspoon ground cinnamon*

In a small bowl, stir together the Yogurt Cheese and dates. Form the mixture into a disk or a log. In a small cup, stir together the sugar and cinnamon and sprinkle the mixture over the surface of the cheese.
   Makes approximately 1⅓ cups

PEPPERED HERB YOGURT CHEESE

1 recipe of Plain Yogurt Cheese
Freshly ground black pepper

Assorted fresh and dried herbs such as
basil, dill, oregano, parsley, rosemary,
sage, and thyme

Form the Yogurt Cheese into a disk or a log and season with the pepper and herbs as desired. Or, alternatively, stir all the ingredients together and serve in a pot or small bowl.

Makes approximately 1 cup

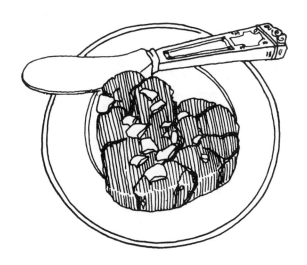

The Perfect Tea

Teatime

While you can serve scones at any time of day, scones are a must at tea. Teas are booming in the United States. Prestigious hotels and restaurants are offering tea. And, in some cases, the "power tea" is replacing the "power lunch." Americans have gotten used to eating (or grazing) all day long and "happy hours" are on the wane. Scones and other tea fare provide the perfect antidote to hunger pangs between lunch and a late dinner.

Anna, the seventh Duchess of Bedford, is credited as the creator of teatime. During the middle of the eighteenth century, dinner for the upper and middle classes had shifted from noontime to an evening meal that was served at a fashionably late hour. Because the noon meal had become skimpier, the Duchess suffered from "a sinking feeling" at about four o'clock in the afternoon. At first the Duchess had her servants sneak a pot of tea and a few breadstuffs into her dressing room. But soon, she came out of the closet. Once she had moved out into the open, many of her friends joined her, and tea became a way of life among the royalty in England.

Teatime is when you should take the opportunity to pamper yourself and your guests. Set the table with your finest or favorite tableware. Teapots are made of a variety of materials. The best ones to use are made of china, earthenware, glass, silver, or stainless steel. You can set the mood for the afternoon respite by the type of tea service that you use. Boldly patterned high-tech teapots have become common in the marketplace, and many of them have been designed by contemporary architects. Traditional delicate floral bone china and an antique lace tablecloth would present an entirely different feel. Miniature tea sets are great fun for children, and afternoon tea can provide the perfect classroom for those first lessons in good manners.

Whether you are in a formal dining room or under the old oak tree, the setting for tea is also important. Taking a tea break at your desk can provide a bright spot during a day filled with too much work. No matter whether you have time for just a cup of tea and a scone or two or are partaking of a full-blown affair, teatime is definitely a civilized tradition that more and more Americans are making a habit.

There are several ways that the English enjoy tea. Sometimes they just have time for "a cuppa." Other teas include small tea sandwiches and assorted baked goods such as scones, biscuits, and cakes. High tea consists of much heartier fare and often includes meat dishes. In many cases, high tea provides a substitute for dinner. Children are often given high tea fare for their dinner and the adults enjoy a late dinner. Whichever way you take your tea, it's the American way to build on tradition and we've certainly taken liberties! We don't think there's an English person out there who would have ever put sun-dried tomatoes in anything related to a scone! (See Uptown Scones, page 101).

By the way, many of our spreads work well in tea sandwiches. Classically, tea sandwiches are nearly always crustless and closed rather than open-faced, but don't hesitate to experiment and create your own style. If you can't serve the sandwiches right away, arrange them on a serving tray or plate and cover them with a damp, well-wrung-out dish towel for up to two hours. Try the Chutney Cream Cheese (page 107) on thinly sliced crustless whole-wheat bread and sandwich it with thin slices of apple for crunch.

• TEA FOR TWO—OR MORE •

The Chinese are credited with discovering tea. Around 2700 B.C., Emperor Shen Nung was brewing his customary drink of boiled water when leaves from an overhanging tea tree accidentally fell into the kettle.

Tea is the world's most popular beverage next to water. The United States is second only to Great Britain in the amount of tea consumed each day by its people. Americans drink an average of 46 billion servings of tea each year and about 37 billion of these are iced tea. Over 200 million pounds of tea are imported into the United States each year.

Iced tea was born in 1904 in St. Louis. Richard Blechynden of Calcutta was representing teas from the Far East at the Louisiana Purchase Exposition Fair. Because the weather was stifling hot and everyone was passing his booth, he iced the tea and his stand gained instant popularity! It was in this same year that teabags were introduced. Thomas Sullivan was a tea and coffee merchant in New York and he sent samples to customers in small tins. He decided that it would be easier and less expensive to put tea in bags instead. So he ordered one hundred little silk hand-sewn bags and filled them with tea. After people discovered the convenience of these bags, orders began to pour in for tea packaged in the little bags. In the U.S. today, more than half of the tea drunk is made with teabags.

• BREWING THE PERFECT POT OF TEA •

There is much debate about the way tea should and should not be made, and, of course, much of this debate occurs during teatime. There is also much discussion as to whether tea should be served with cream, milk, sugar, or lemon. And to complicate this even further, whether you add cold milk (the British seem to agree that the milk should be cold) *before* or *after* you add tea seems also to be a popular controversy.

Tea should be stored in a cool, dry, airtight container (*not* in the refrigerator or freezer). Rinse your teapot with hot water and let the water stand in the pot for a few minutes to warm the container. This will keep the tea hot during the brewing. Run the tap water for your tea for several seconds so that it will be fresh and aerated (aeration brings out the full character of the tea). Always start with cold water as hot water may have stagnated in the pipes for too long and water that is reheated gives the tea a flat taste. Bring the fresh cold tap water to a full rolling boil. Only boiling water can extract the full flavor from the tea leaves. When filling the teapot, bring the pot to the kettle to keep the water as hot as possible. Use one teaspoonful or 1 teabag per five-ounce cup and pour the boiling water directly over the tea. Some say to add an extra teaspoon or bag "for the pot." Cover the pot and let the tea brew for three to five minutes—color is not an accurate guide for doneness. It takes time for the leaves to unfold and release their flavor. (If you like tea that is less strong, add water after brewing.) Stir the tea and strain it, if necessary, into the cups. Add cream, milk, sugar, or lemon as you fancy.

◆ FOR ICED TEA ◆

Use fifty percent more tea to allow for melting ice. For example, you need four teabags to make four cups of hot tea. For iced tea, you need six teabags to make four glasses of tea. To make a two-quart pitcherful, bring one quart of freshly drawn cold water to a full rolling boil in a saucepan. Remove the pan from the heat and add fifteen teabags or one-third cup of loose tea. Stir, cover, and let stand for five minutes. Remove the teabags or strain. Do not refrigerate. Keep at room temperature and pour over ice when ready to serve.

◆ FOR SUN TEA ◆

Fill a quart pitcher or container with cold tap water. Add 8 to 10 teabags (remove tags). Cover and let stand at room temperature, in the sun or in the refrigerator for at least 6 hours or overnight. Remove the teabags, squeezing them against the side of the container. Keep covered and refrigerated. When ready to serve, pour into ice-filled glasses.

(The previous tea-making information comes from the Tea Council of the U.S.A., Inc.)

One thing we do know, Henry Fielding was right when he said back in the 1700s, "Love and scandal are the best sweeteners of tea."

Index